Gardening
the Bhakti yoga way

A gardening therapy book

Brian Bhakti McCulloch

PIPIT

First published in Great Britain in 2022 by Pipit Books

Contents

Acknowledgements

Thanks to Jan, Mica, Ami, Sam, Lesley, Zeb, Claire, Meg, Mark, Andy, Saranga Thakura Dasa, Phil, Berta, Ramananda Dasa, Palika Devi, and Palika's mother Margret for helping with finances. Ratnaranjini devi. My gardening guru Geoff Hamilton, Mark, and Lisa. This book was inspired by *Bhagavada-Gītā as it is* by His Divine Grace A.C. Bhaktivedanta swami Prabhupada. I would also like to thank my legs for supporting me; my arms, they were always by my side, and my fingers, I could always count on them.

Foreword

In his first book Brian McCulloch, a.k.a Bhaktivinode das, avid gardener, pioneer of horticultural therapy and one of the leaders of the Hare Krishna community in Scotland, provides us with a book that is both practical and philosophical, and that connects ancient yoga texts with organic fruit and vegetable production.

Amid current concerns about food security, food sovereignty and climate change, this book humbly proffers sound gardening advice from the voice of experience; someone with their hands in the soil who has spent nearly all of their life growing food, serving it to Krishna, sharing it with the world and sharing it with love. Very readable, a wonderful blend of memoir, anecdote and theological insight; there is no gardening book like this one!

Stephen Shaw

Garden Team Leader

Krishna Eco Farm

Introduction

I hope the reader will experience some of the inner enjoyment I've experienced while growing, harvesting, offering and eating fruit, vegetables and flowers.

This is a gardening book with a difference.

The difference between this gardening book and others is that I have included Krishna in this gardening book. Who is Krishna? The name Krishna means all attractive.

*Isvara parama krsna sac cid ananda vigrahah anadir
adir govinda sarva karana karanam.*

"Krishna who is known as Govinda is the supreme personality of godhead. He has an eternal, blissful, spiritual body. He is the origin of all, he has no origin, he is the prime cause of all causes."

We approach Krishna through the process of Bhakti yoga. *Yoga* means to link, so *Bhakti*, or devotion, means that we link up with Krishna through love and devotion. Anyone can begin Bhakti yoga simply by offering a leaf, a flower, some fruit or even a little water to Krishna. Krishna Himself says in the Bhagavad-gītā, Chapter 9, text 26: "If one offers me, with love and devotion, a leaf, a flower, a fruit or water, I will accept it."

You don't even need to have a garden to practice the yoga described in this book, you can simply grow a few plants on your window ledge. If you have a big window ledge you can grow tomatoes and peppers; if you have a small window ledge you can grow herbs like coriander as well as small flowers like hyacinths, but it is always essential to have a sunny window ledge. This is a very easy way to practice Bhakti yoga, all you have to do is offer whatever the plant produces to Krishna, with love and devotion. If you offer your produce to Krishna in this mood of love, then Krishna will accept it and your produce will be spiritualised. If you offer your hyacinths, then you can relate to Krishna by the fragrance of the flower. Krishna says in the Bhagavad-gītā, Chapter 7, text 9: "I am the original fragrance of the earth." So we can relate to Krishna by connecting the fragrance of the flower to Krishna's personality. Hyacinths have a very beautiful fragrance so we can understand that Krishna is a very beautiful person by the fragrance of the hyacinth flowers.

We can cook the tomatoes and peppers for a pizza or in a vegetable dish, and we can offer the preparation to Krishna with love and devotion. Love and devotion means to follow proper standards of cleanliness and to cook properly; we should also use the proper mantras, or prayers, to offer the produce. It is important to be in the mood to try to please Krishna and His devotees whilst cooking. After we have offered the preparation, we can serve it to our neighbours and guests. This is a great way to make friends and attract others to the yoga of Krishna consciousness.

Even in the more advanced stages of Bhakti yoga we offer our food to Krishna. We should offer Krishna the best that we have to offer, so we should grow as much as we can ourselves. The renowned teacher of Bhakti yoga, A.C. Bhaktivedanta

Swami Prabhupada, or Srila Prabhupada as he is more commonly known, says that home grown food is far superior to that bought in a shop. In one of his books, *the Nectar of Instruction*, he explains that giving and receiving of Prasadam, spiritual food which has been offered to Krishna, is one of the loving exchanges practised between devotees of Krishna. Bhakti yoga is all about love and if we perform this yoga under the guidance of a spiritual master, that divine love will awaken in our hearts, and we will feel for the welfare of all other souls. By practising Bhakti yoga we are doing the topmost welfare work for all living entities and if we offer the produce from our plants to Krishna, the soul in the body of that plant achieves a human form in its next birth. This is the science of reincarnation.

The Bhagavad-gītā explains very clearly the science of reincarnation. Souls do not only live in human bodies, they live in all animal and plant bodies. According to the Bhakti teachings, there are 8,400,000 species of life in the material world, but only in the human form of life can we become conscious of God. A soul in a plant form or in the body of an animal cannot become God conscious. However, in very exceptional circumstances, if we look after a plant and serve the plant with love and devotion the soul within that body may go straight back to the spiritual world; we should always remember that Krishna can do anything.

Bhakti yoga means to be attentive to detail, so look after the plants, serve them with love; after all, they are serving us by providing our food. Make sure you use the proper soil and that your pots are clean, water your plants regularly but not too much and make sure you weed them, even if they are in pots. The aim of this book isn't just to encourage people to grow food and flowers, it is also to encourage people to grow with love and to offer the produce to Krishna. If people grow their food in this way, the love that will emanate from our practice of Bhakti yoga will improve the situation in the world, others will feel that love and go looking for the source of that love. The great gardener George Harrison of The Beatles once wrote that everyone is looking for Krishna, but some do not yet know that they are looking for Him. Love is the most powerful force in the universe. Nothing and nobody can kill love. Krishna tells us in His Bhagavad-gītā, Chapter 2 text 17: "That which pervades the entire body you should know to be indestructible. No one can destroy that imperishable soul." And later in the same chapter, text 23, He says: "The soul can never be cut to pieces by any weapon, nor burned by fire, nor moistened by water, nor withered by the wind." The soul is made of love and to love is our true nature. To use the word love in its proper context we have to add Krishna. Love means to love everyone, including Krishna. Every soul is a part of Krishna, so if we have love for Krishna then we will love plants, animals and all our fellow humans.

By growing our own food and flowers we save a lot of plastic being used. I am noticing in shops now that they are using paper bags and cotton bags since there is a great deal of concern about the environmental impact of plastic waste. The amount of plastic which is being used is ridiculous, there is no room for it all on the planet. It takes lifetimes to break down and if it's burned it causes a lot of pollution and damage to the environment, however if lots of people grow their own fruit, vegetables and flowers then we can cut down on the amount of plastic being used. This is a very serious situation which we have to do something about, we don't want to create bad karma for ourselves by using plastic unnecessarily. It is best to avoid buying food wrapped in plastic as much as possible. I know that Sivarama Swami, a well-known Bhakti yogi and eco campaigner, will be happy that I've mentioned this topic.

Chapter One

Paradise

I put a paradise flower on the front cover of this book because I feel like I'm in paradise when I'm in my garden. Just by looking at all the beautiful colours and seeing the fruit and veg growing, I feel positive and happy. It's such an excellent and natural way to be happy, and I forget all my troubles when I'm in the garden. At that time, I feel that at least some of Planet Earth is beautiful.

Bhakti yoga is meant to make us feel good, positive and happy. Bhakti yoga in the garden is easy; you don't have to be a gymnast. Bhakti yoga is the yoga of love. You are made of love; all you need is love. Everyone has love to give and is looking for love. Love means we love all living beings, including plants. We may sometimes feel that we can't give love or are not worthy of receiving love. The love in our hearts will never completely die, so at any time, we can revive the love in our hearts.

The garden is a great place to cultivate a loving mood towards Mother Earth (Mother Bhumi). Bhumi devi provides us with all the necessities of life, so we should take care of and use the land to serve Bhumi devi. Bhumi devi is a goddess; devi means female servant of Krishna. Krishna is the all-attractive person, and gardens are attractive, so the garden's creator must be attractive. We give the artist who painted a picture of a beautiful flower credit for painting the picture, so we should give the original artist who created the flower credit for creating something so beautiful. I often wonder at how the colours merge into each other on the petals of flowers like poppies. I always take the time to look at how the petals of fuchsias wrap around each other; that's no accident; a beautiful creator created that work of art. I also love the fragrance of some flowers. The night-scented stock makes me feel like I'm in paradise in the garden. Not only can we have a beautiful-looking garden, but we can have charming fragrances in the garden. Hyacinths also have a beautiful scent in early spring, so with the garden looking beautiful, the fragrances heighten the mood.

I urge you to grow the Bhakti yoga way. It is essential for ourselves and for the planet. There may come a time when we will have to grow our own food to eat. So we should start now. When we grow, we can make the extra effort to offer the produce to Krishna. If we offer the garden produce to Krishna, the love we do the service with will improve the situation in the world. We can all afford the best, and we can all afford Krishna. All Krishna is looking for is love; go for it, and you'll be surprised. The soul's deepest desire is to love and to be loved, so why not go for the best?

An essential part of Bhakti yoga is to love yourself. To love ourselves, we have to know who we are. We're souls, and we're indestructible; we're eternal; we can't be burned, dried, moistened by water, nor withered by the wind. We're part and parcel of Krishna, the supreme being. So when we know who we are, we become fearless. An excellent way to start loving ourselves and the plants is to chant the Maha-Mantra out loud to our plants in the garden. The Maha-Mantra is Hare Krishna Hare Krishna Krishna Krishna Hare Hare Hare Rama Hare Rama Rama Rama Hare Hare.

If we love ourselves, we can love others because we'll know who others are. So an excellent way to love our plants is to chant Hare Krishna to them.

Yoga is all about love. There was once a great saint called Haridasa Thakura who advised us to chant the Maha-Mantra to the non-moving living entities like trees. That way, we're showing the most incredible love to the plants. There are different types of yoga; we call it the yoga ladder. Bhakti yoga is the topmost yoga, and we don't need to practice any other yoga if we practice Bhakti yoga. However, we can practice different types of yoga if we want to; that is a personal choice, and other forms of yoga can complement Bhakti yoga. The goal of yoga is to love God, and a great place to learn to love God is in the garden. You may ask, "Does God exist? How do I find out if there is a God?"

I'm writing this book because I've found God in the garden. So I'm giving you a chance to meet your maker before you die, then you can die peacefully. It's intelligent to think there's an intelligent person behind the creation of a garden; I plant the seeds, but I don't make it rain, and I don't make the Sunshine. I go through specific procedures to grow flowers, fruit and veg. I don't just wait and see if flowers appear in my garden by accident. For plants to grow, they need rain and Sun, so God has arranged for the plants to be watered in the form of rain and for the Sun to shine to help the plants grow. So there's an arrangement for the plants to grow in certain conditions. It's intelligent to conclude that if arrangements are being made, a person is making those arrangements. It's also wise to conclude that if the creation is beautiful, then the creator is beautiful. Demigods like the Sun god make arrangements in the material world, and the Moon god, Candra, also participates in the growing process. Bhagavad-gita states that the Moon gives the vegetables the juice of life. The demigods can't do anything without being empowered by Krishna. So we can show appreciation to God for creating beautiful fragrant flowers and tasty fruit and veg by chanting Hare Krishna to the plants. We can also offer the produce from the garden to Krishna; we can offer flowers to pictures of saints or decorate our altar with flowers from the garden. We can also make juice from the fruit we pick from the garden and offer it. We can also pick lovely fruit and veg like apples and potatoes and make apple crumble and chips and offer them to Krishna. I love serving steamed potatoes from the garden to guests, and I also love eating them too. There's so much enjoyment in growing fruit, veg and flowers and offering them, serving them and eating them; that's why I've given detailed guidelines on how to offer produce from the garden to Krishna. So if you don't know that Krishna is God, try offering produce from the garden and taste the offered food (prasadam). So many people eat Krishna food and say it is amazingly wonderful. The food takes on a spiritual aspect when we offer it. You won't be disappointed if you offer the produce with love and devotion.

In Bhakti yoga, service is joyfully performed. We should also be enthusiastic when serving, and enthusiasm is infectious. If we're enthusiastic, others around us and helping us will also become enthusiastic. There's no stopping someone who is enthusiastic. If someone who's helping us isn't doing very well and we're enthusiastic, it may just pull them through. I'm sure everyone reading this has experienced difficulties in life. Some people can't cope and end up in a terrible state or even commit suicide.

Gardening can be great therapy, especially if we add Krishna. By adding Krishna, our love is complete. We all have love to give, but are we all satisfied and happy inside? If we add Krishna to our gardening, we will be happy inside; we can live on the basic necessities of life if we're spiritually happy. My motto is simple living, peace of mind and high thinking.

I once took part in a horticultural therapy course, and it was amazing; I wish the whole world would take part in horticultural therapy. I'm trying to encourage as many people as possible to participate; that's why I'm writing this book. It's very practical to grow. Growing fruit, veg or flowers is good for the body, mind and soul. We can keep physically fit by getting exercise digging and making compost, we can get over mental problems by feeling positive when we see plants grow, we forget our problems when we're enthusiastic, and we give the soul the vitamin called love when we appreciate God in the garden and when we eat the prasadam (food offered to Krishna). We must start growing for our own sakes, even if it's just a few plants on a window ledge.

Bhakti yoga in the garden is easy, all we need is love, and we've all got love in our hearts, so everyone is qualified to start practising Bhakti yoga. We can start by growing a few flowers that are easy to grow, like marigolds and cornflowers. Marigolds and cornflowers can be used to make beautiful garlands and as decorations around pictures. Marigolds and cornflowers also make any veg patch look attractive if we dot them around the patch. I love being creative in the garden; I sprinkle marigolds and cornflowers around my veg patch and create an ornamental kitchen garden.

Marigolds and cornflowers take little time to grow; sowing

the seed to picking the flowers can take just two months. All we need is a few seed trays that can be bought in any garden centre, some compost, seeds, and a watering can with a fine rose. From January to May, you can sow the seeds; if you have a heated propagator, you can start in January; if you're putting the trays on a sunny window ledge, sow the seeds in March or April. Fill the seed tray with compost, firm the compost down with your hand, leave a half-inch gap at the top of the tray, sprinkle about thirty seeds on each tray, and cover the seeds with a thin layer of compost. Water with a watering can with a fine rose suitable for watering seeds. Start watering off the tray; then, when you have a fine shower of water, move back and forward over the tray for about 20 seconds. Leave the tray to drain, then put the trays on a sunny window ledge or in a propagator. Water the seeds every two or three days, and keep the compost moist. It might be better to take the trays outdoors to water them. When the seedlings are about four weeks old and have four leaves, put them in a cold frame, or if it's warm enough, plant them directly into the ground in the garden. Be careful of late frosts; I've lost plants in mid-May due to frost. It is always good to have a tray or two of seedlings as a backup. I usually plant seedlings from the tray to the garden about six to eight weeks after sowing. Ensure the garden soil is well dug over and rich in compost. You can also add well-rotted cow dung to the ground five months before planting the flowers. Cornflowers and marigolds will produce flowers quickly, and you may have to support cornflowers with a cane.

Pick the first marigolds from the centre of the flowers so the plant bushes out and produces more flowers. Daffodils and tulips make a beautiful spring display; plant the bulbs twice the depth of the bulb in October or November, and add horticultural sand if you have clay soil. Then all you have to do is wait until the bulbs produce flowers, and then you can appreciate that Krishna is the flower-bearing spring. Bhagavad-gītā Chapter 10, verse 35, states, "Of the hymns in the Sama Veda, I am the brhat sama, and of poetry, I am the Gayatri. Of months I am Magrasira (November December), and of seasons I am the flower-bearing spring." After winter, it's so nice to see colour in the garden. I love to see snowdrops and colourful crocuses in February and March. It's always worthwhile to make an effort to plant bulbs in October and November.

This is a gardening therapy book, so the book aims to make the reader happy. The spiritual world is full of flowers and is very beautiful, so we can get a hint of the beauty of the spiritual world by seeing a beautiful garden. While practising Bhakti yoga, we enjoy within, which means we appreciate the creator, Krishna, while we're in the garden, and we offer the fruit, veg and flowers we grow to Krishna.

Gardening the Bhakti yoga way can help us see that God is an attractive person. The word Krishna means all attractive. Krishna is often seen with flower garlands around his neck and likes spending time in the garden with his lady friends. Krishna is the supreme enjoyer and wants us to take part in his pastimes, so by offering the garden produce to Krishna and appreciating Krishna in the garden by seeing the beauty, and relating the fragrances of flowers to Krishna, we are taking part in Radha (Krishna's favourite lady friend) and Krishna's pastimes. The idea is to heighten Radha and Krishna's enjoyment. Love means to perform activities for others without wanting anything in return for ourselves; in fact, the reward for serving Radha and Krishna is more service, so Bhakti yoga can solve the unemployment problem in the world. If we're enthusiastic about growing the Bhakti yoga way, Krishna will make sure we always have some service.

As a gardener, I'm always employed; I can always find some gardening, even if it's just for bed and board. I've worked on many fruit and veg farms, sometimes just for bed and board and to get hands-on experience. The best way to learn gardening is to get hands-on experience; there's no better way to learn gardening than to work with an enthusiastic gardener. This book aims to encourage people to grow for Krishna; I've given simple, straightforward guidelines to help you get started. I've written in a way that expresses the enjoyment I get from gardening the Bhakti yoga way.

If we enjoy gardening the Bhakti yoga way, we can rise above many problems and keep physically fit; we can improve our mental health by regulating our lives. Being in a beautiful environment can also help; we can feel positive when we see plants grow and be happy when we pick flowers, fruit and veg. We can improve our spiritual health by appreciating Krishna in the garden and offering the produce to Krishna. Gardening the Bhakti yoga way has helped me get over many problems. Once, I came across a ghost in the garden, they do exist, but due to being in a beautiful environment and being with friendly, supportive people, I was even able to help the ghost who was looking for help; I just chanted Hare Krishna to the ghost, and she picked up my loving mood towards her and moved into another gross body. True story, don't doubt me. If you come across a ghost who won't reciprocate with our love, then we chant the Nrsimhadeva mantras in this book; those mantras will scare the ghost away.

Practising Bhakti yoga helps us cultivate compassion, and compassion means we help souls who are less fortunate than us. Ghosts are jivas who have left their gross bodies and are trapped in subtle bodies. We can detect ghosts by detecting an unusual disturbance in our minds and a heavy mood of ignorance. We can be compassionate to ghosts and souls in plant bodies. There's a lot of suffering in the world, so by practising Bhakti yoga in the garden, we create a loving mood in the garden that affects the whole world and improves the situation in the world. If we give love out to the world, someone will pick up on that love and go looking for the source of that love. If someone is looking for the source of love, Krishna in the heart will direct a searching soul to a person who wants to lead souls to Krishna. The perfection of Bhakti yoga means we love all living beings, be they in human or animal bodies or plant bodies. Souls in human bodies tend to think they are more important than souls in animal or plant bodies. Animals and plants have as much right to live on this planet as humans; we couldn't breathe without trees, insects pollinate plants, and cow dung is an excellent fertiliser. There's an amazing interaction of souls in different species, all cooperating to give us pleasure. That perfect arrangement is set into motion by Krishna. Krishna is the reservoir of all pleasure.

The social aspect of gardening is very important; it's not much fun gardening on our own. Even if we garden on our own, we like to sit in the garden with friends, and we're happy if our visitors enjoy our garden. I also like serving meals to visitors while we're sitting in the garden. Bhakti yoga is about serving and pleasing others, so an excellent way to please others is to serve them fruit juice made from fruit from the garden while sitting in the garden. A great way to impress friends is to grow, harvest, cook and offer the preparation to Krishna, then serve the meal with a smile to others sitting in the garden. You can still benefit from gardening the Bhakti yoga way if you are on your own for whatever reason; if you add Krishna to your gardening, you won't feel lonely; Krishna is in your heart and will reciprocate with your love and devotion.

Another great way to please neighbours is to have a window box full of very colourful, attractive flowers or make hanging baskets and hang them outside the door. I always appreciate seeing hanging baskets and window boxes along a street. I also like to see railway stations with lots of colourful flower displays. I remember we went to Wemyss Bay train station in Scotland on our way to Rothesay on the Isle of Bute. Seeing such a lovely flower display in the station was so nice. I was very impressed by the park in Rothesay, too. It's very satisfying to see lovely flower displays in parks.

I'll never forget that trip to Rothesay; we walked to Ardengraig garden council. It was a delightful walk from the town of Rothesay along the seashore and up the hill to the garden. The garden was in full bloom, and it was the middle of September in Scotland. They say a warm current of water called the gulf stream flows past The Isle of Bute, so the temperature there is slightly warmer than on the mainland. Hence, the growing season is somewhat longer on Rothsay compared to the mainland. We were lucky enough to meet the gardener while looking around the garden, so we chatted. I told him how impressed I was with the garden, so he was happy to talk for a while. I gave him a book on Bhakti yoga called "chant and be happy"; in the book is an interview with George Harrison, a very keen gardener. The gardener was telling me that he was going to start doing horticultural therapy to help local people. It's far better to go out to a garden, meet others, and do some gardening than sit in a house and ruminate on problems. Horticultural therapy can help people with all sorts of issues. If one is unemployed, it can help by keeping us busy and positive and can lead to paid work. If we're lonely, gardening can help us if we go out and mix with people in the garden. Gardens are great places to cultivate friendships. If we're gardening with friendly, supportive people, that can help us rise above depression, and if we garden the Bhakti yoga way, that can help us transcend anxiety.

George Harrison says everyone is looking for Krishna; some just don't know they are looking for Krishna. Gardening the Bhakti yoga way helps us find Krishna. The benefits of gardening the Bhakti yoga way are limitless, and there's no ceiling to the happiness we can experience while doing Bhakti yoga. Bob Marley sang, "I'm happy inside", we should be happy inside; if we're not, try a bit of Bhakti yoga in the garden. Bob also sang "satisfy my soul", we can satisfy our souls by doing Bhakti yoga in the garden.

Krishna's satisfaction is our satisfaction, so if we make a beautiful garden for Krishna's pleasure and offer the fruit, veg and flowers from the garden, Krishna will be satisfied with us, so we can feel satisfaction because we've done something for Krishna. Of course, we don't just rest on our laurels after a bit of Bhakti yoga in the garden, we can constantly improve, and in one sense, we should always feel we can do better, so we're satisfied because we're serving Krishna, at the same time we're not satisfied, because we know we can always do better.

It's easy to make friends while gardening the Bhakti yoga way because we have a common mood of gardening with love with our fellow gardeners. The aim of Bhakti yoga in the garden is to cultivate love for the souls in the bodies of the plants. Flowers make the world beautiful, and the fragrances of some flowers are marvellous. Plants provide us with a great variety of fruit and veg that we can offer to Krishna and serve to others, so why not love the plants? I've made many friends by growing fruit and veg, cooking fruit and veg, offering it to Krishna, and then serving the preparations to my guests. Many people are very impressed by the taste of fresh fruit and veg recently picked from the garden. Bhakti yoga is joyfully performed. We all have it in us to serve and please others, so we can be motivated to grow and serve if the end result is that many people are pleased with your meals from the garden. As time goes by, we can grow in confidence and even become famous for our wonderful meals. People from all over the world come to the Krishna eco farm in Scotland, so I get the chance to serve many people meals from the garden. I don't serve meals to become famous, but Krishna food is very famous. The international society for Krishna consciousness has farms and restaurants worldwide. Practically everyone who visits the eco farm here in Scotland comments on how good the food is here; that's why I've given directions on how to grow, offer and serve produce from the garden.

By growing the Bhakti yoga way, we cultivate the creeper of devotion in our hearts. When we start Bhakti yoga, Krishna plants a seed of love in our hearts. So just like we cultivate seedlings in the garden, we develop the seedling of love in our hearts. We water the seedling of love in our hearts by serving plants the Bhakti yoga way. If we weed the garden for Krishna's pleasure, then every weed we pull up will be like pulling a material desire from our hearts. Let's look after the seedling of love in our hearts. It will quickly grow and break through the material realm, reach the spiritual realm, and eventually reach the lotus feet of Krishna, where it will bloom. We generally make gradual progress when practising Bhakti yoga, so we have to be patient. We must be patient and give the plants in the garden and the plants in our hearts time to grow. Even if we practice Bhakti yoga in the garden, we're generally living in a grey area of material and spiritual, so we give the yoga time to work and make gradual progress and come out of the darkness and into the light. At the same time, we can become fully Krishna-conscious in a moment; that's very rare but possible. The goal of Bhakti yoga is to become fully Krishna-conscious, which means we love all living beings. I hope I've helped you, the reader, on your journey to find out what life is all about. Lots of love from Bhakti. I'm happy to write that Bhakti is my middle name.

Chapter Two

Making spiritual advancement in the garden

I am not claiming to be the world's best gardener. The aim of this book is to encourage people to offer the produce from their garden to Krishna and in that way one can make spiritual advancement. If we offer our produce to Krishna with love and devotion, then all living entities will benefit. I do, however, love gardening and I want to share my wonderful gardening experiences with others, since it's an activity that is so enjoyable and rewarding. When I go out to the garden, to dig up potatoes, or pick fruit, I think that the money I have in the bank is staying there because I won't have to buy any fruit or potatoes that day.

Growing food and flowers is a great way to appreciate Krishna, God, and to appreciate the plants which He has given. Just think how many apples an apple tree can produce; plants are doing us a great service by providing us with our fruit and vegetables. They also make the world more beautiful by their colourful flowers and beautiful fragrances, so we can thank them and serve them by offering what they produce to Krishna. It's so nice to go out to the garden, pick flowers and offer them to Krishna. It is so satisfying to see an altar, or shrine, decorated with flowers grown from the garden. Krishna is so amazing that he creates such a variety of different colours. God is not a boring person.

There is a terrible problem in the world with boredom. Many

people are bored from doing the same mundane activities every day. If we take up Bhakti yoga by growing plants and offering the produce to Krishna, we will never be bored. There will always be something to do, something to talk about and something to be enthusiastic about. We will have to think about what to grow, where to grow it and how to look after the plants properly; we can treat our plants just like our children.

I remember one morning I got up very early in the morning just to water my plants. I had been thinking of a friend of mine, Kirsten, who I used to garden with, and it was to please her that I had got up and watered them. Sometimes life gets us down and we cannot think of a reason to get up, but if we grow plants and act like a loving parent towards them and serve the plants in this way then that will give us a reason to get up in the morning.

Growing plants is also a good way to regulate our lives. If we sow seeds then we have to water them in the morning and in the evening. We have to weed them and feed them. Any mental health practitioner, or serious practitioner of spiritual life, will tell you how important it is to regulate your day. One lady once told me to regulate, celebrate and make the most of the good times. We can do that in the garden. We can regulate by looking after our plants properly. We can celebrate when the plants produce. And we can make the most of the good times by offering the food we have grown to Krishna and then honour that food by our eating.

Everyone's a winner when it comes to Bhakti yoga. A little bit of service in Bhakti frees one from the most dangerous type of fear. As Krishna says in the Bhagavad-gītā, Chapter 2, text 40: "In this endeavour there is no loss or diminution, and a little advancement on this path can free one from the most danger-ous type of fear."

It is never too late. We can begin gardening for Krishna at a very young age, but even if your body is older you can still grow some plants and please Krishna by offering the produce. The benefits of Bhakti yoga are unlimited. We are eternal souls and there is no ceiling to the happiness we can experience in spiritual life. So, we can begin by growing a few plants and end up in the spiritual world in a very short time. Srila Prabhupada states that one can become Krishna conscious in a moment, so who knows? You might attain liberation just by offering some flowers, or some apples, or some tomatoes to Krishna. That's very rare, however. Remember that Bhakti yoga is a gradual process, we generally make gradual advancement, so we need to be patient. We have to be careful not to water too much, or feed too much, or use soil that is too rich. If we try to hurry things too much, then we can kill our plants.

Gardening is great therapy. It can help with anxiety, depres-sion and stress. I'm sure my good friend Jan Cameron, a professional horticultural therapist, will back me up on that. Gardening the Bhakti yoga way is good for body, mind and soul. I haven't just sat down to write this book on a whim. My whole life revolves around growing fruit, vegetables and flowers and has done for many years. This book is my attempt to get across to people how enjoyable and fun gardening can be for people of all ages. Even a few small pots on a window ledge or box, a hanging basket at our door, or a small growing patch out in our back garden can make such a big difference to our lives. If we garden with other people we can become much more enthusiastic and positive about our life, and we can cultivate deep friendships. We can also realise that plants are sentient beings, just like us.

Plants are very beautiful; they offer a very nice fragrance, and they produce food for us. That is more than I can say for some human beings! Lots of plants make a real addition to the earth, while humans can sometimes be very destructive. If we offer our flowers, fruit, and vegetables to Krishna with love and devotion, and if we share the meals we make from them with others we can quickly realise who we really are and who Krishna is. That is not difficult, Krishna consciousness is deceptively simple. Even if you do not believe in God you can still benefit from this book. Put it to the test, try offering your food to Krishna by following the guidelines set out here. If you follow the instructions about offering food, then you will experience the love of Bhakti yoga. The proof of the pudding is in the eating. You won't be disappointed.

We can see that there are many arrangements being made in the world. We can order something online and it is delivered to our doors. There are people making those arrangements. Similarly for food to grow there are arrangements being made; the sun shines, the clouds pour rain. So, it is common sense to conclude that there is some intelligence behind everything. According to the ancient yoga teachings, there are powerful beings, demigods, who are in charge of managing the material world. These demigods can't do anything without becoming empowered by Krishna, the Supreme Personality of Godhead. We call nature our mother because we are being looked after by her. Some say God is the father because he provides and protects. We can also say Krishna is our mother because the soft loving aspect of Krishna's nature is there too. We can become conscious of Krishna's nature by respecting and serving the souls in the bodies of plants. These souls are also devotees of Krishna and if we offer to Him the flowers, fruits and vegetables of those plants which we are cultivating then the souls in those plant bodies receive a human form in their next birth. So, we are rendering the highest service to the souls in the plant bodies. In the human form we can solve all our problems by this process of yoga; plants and animals cannot do that. We can attain love of God only in human form. At such a level of spiritual realisation we will understand that we don't own anything, everything belongs to Krishna. There will be no more problems in life at such a stage of consciousness. Of course, we will always have our everyday problems, like paying the rent, but in the highest stage of Krishna consciousness all we will have is love. We've got to start somewhere, and a good way to start Bhakti yoga is to grow plants and offer the produce to Krishna.

Gardening as recreation can help the earth. My nature is to serve and any financial profit from this book will be used to help improve the situation in the world. So much soil has been burned out on this planet, in some places they say we've only got sixty years of growing left. If we keep busy serving others then we will forget our own problems and struggles. Those who assist us will forget their problems also.

This book is my offering to the world. I want to give as many people as possible the chance to practice Bhakti yoga. I am doing this as a service to Mother Bhumi, Mother earth. There is a lot of concern about the chemicals used on food but if we grow our own food in our own gardens and allotments and in community gardens then we can make a difference. Pests, insects and so on are a problem but if we can grow enough food for ourselves and for the pests then that will make a difference. In all my years of growing I have never had all my plants wiped out by pests, it has always been worthwhile growing, and it has also saved me a lot of money. Still, we can take precautions regarding pests, and I have written about that in this book.

I don't claim to be a big producing farmer, that is not my department, although I am very interested in it since it is the future of the planet. I am sure that there are experts on growing organic food on a large scale. I am just an insignificant soul trying to encourage others to grow something and to offer it to Krishna. If we can grow with love, then that love will go out to the world and lift people's spirits. No one can cancel your love. We just have to garden the Bhakti yoga way and our disease of material life will be cured. We have the chance to solve all our problems while we are in our human form. It is said that we are not actually human if we do not inquire about how to solve our problems. There are people with arms and legs that look like humans but don't actually behave like humans. Humans can be very beautiful if they link up with Krishna. It is not difficult, in fact it is a very pleasant experience eating the produce from a garden after it has been offered to Krishna. Don't forget that service is joyfully performed. If you need some support and encouragement then there are plenty of Krishna farms around the world that would be more than happy if you went along and helped out on the land. There are plenty of opportunities on Krishna Eco Farms to learn how to grow food and flowers.

There are plenty of community gardens and allotment sites that anyone can take part in. By far the best way to learn gardening is hands on, work on the land, and work with someone who is enthusiastic about growing. I just hope this book encourages people to garden with love. I have given guidelines on how to grow and I hope that this will help people start up growing their own produce. It doesn't take much to grow a few plants on a window ledge or to grow on a small plot out the back garden, and hanging baskets or window boxes can make a house more beautiful, and cheer people up.

Happy gardening! I wish you all the best on your journey back to the eternal garden in the spiritual world, where we all belong. The kingdom of God is our rightful inheritance, and our father is a wealthy man. So please take full advantage of this book, enjoy your life, and serve as many plants as you can by engaging them in Krishna's service.

Chapter Three

Be enthusiastic about growing plants

This book will help us in our personal relationships with others because all living beings are related to Krishna. When I was fifteen years old, I remember thinking that there must be more to a person's life than growing up, going off to a war and dying at eighteen. I thought I must be related to all people in some way, so it was a relief to find out the truth about the soul. When I was twenty, I first went to a Krishna temple and I realised that we are all souls, we are all part of Krishna's family.

I am enthusiastic about growing fruit, vegetables and flowers and offering them to Krishna. Gardening the Bhakti yoga way is good for body, mind and soul. It is good for the body because it keeps you physically fit, it is good for the mind because it is productive and it makes us feel positive about life, and it is good for the soul because we offer the produce to Krishna. We are also serving Bhumi-Devi (Mother Earth) if we grow nice fruit, vegetables and flowers and offer them to Krishna. Bhumi-Devi is a person and she is a devotee of Krishna, so if we please Bhumi-Devi then we are pleasing Krishna. A quick way to please Krishna is to please his devotees, just like we say "love me, love my dog".

We can make the world more beautiful by growing flowers. If we decorate our altar at home with nice flowers which we have grown in our garden that will make the home a bit more like the spiritual world. Growing fruit, vegetables and flowers is a lot of fun and at the same time it is very productive. It is also an easy way to make spiritual advancement. The future of the world depends upon humans growing food. In these days of cars, laptops and offices, some people don't get much exercise, so gardening the Bhakti yoga way can help to keep us fit and at the same time we will produce top quality food which will save us money; it is all a gain.

Recently I was passing one Christian lady's garden and she happened to be on her knees, doing some weeding, so I said to her "they say you'll never be closer to God than in your garden." She replied, "yes, that's because you're always on your knees!" It's nice to have a sense of humour. I was watching one popular comedy program on TV. A group of people were going through the countryside and God appeared in the clouds above them and they all got on their knees and asked God to forgive them. God said to them, "I wish someone would tell me a joke sometime, everybody gets on their knees and asks for forgiveness as soon as they see me." So, remember that God is a person, and He has a sense of humour, so we are all in with a chance. Don't forget that a little bit of love makes up for a lot. Krishna is providing everything for us, He is the seed-giving father, He created the Sun, and He makes the clouds pour rain. He created the earth with all the nutrients that we need. When we grow food or flowers, we have to follow a certain procedure: we prepare the soil, we add compost or cow dung, we plant the seed at a certain time of the year and we water the seed. We also make sure we weed around the plants we're cultivating. We make arrangements so that the fruits, vegetables and flowers will grow. It's not that one day we go out to the garden and there are fruits, vegetables and flowers that have just appeared by accident. You don't buy a stick of dynamite and throw it into the garden and expect order to come out of it, and in the same way we won't create a beautiful productive garden by causing an explosion! It may seem crazy to write that, but some people suggest that all of the order in the universe came from a big bang, yet we can see that there are actually arrangements taking place for fruits, vegetables and flowers to grow nicely. Krishna has made an arrangement by creating the Sun and the Moon.

The Moon gives the vegetables the juice of life. The Bhagavad-gītā states in Chapter 15, text 13:

> gām āviśya ca bhūtāni
> dhārayāmy aham ojasā
> puṣṇāmi cauṣadhīḥ sarvāḥ
> somo bhūtvā rasātmakaḥ

"I enter into each planet, and by my energy they stay in orbit. I become the Moon and thereby supply the juice of life to all vegetables."

Who knew that the Moon gives the vegetables the juice of life? I didn't until I'd read the Bhagavad-gītā. Ancient books like the Bhagavad-gītā give us a lot of amazing facts about all aspects of life. Vegetables like beetroot, parsnips and carrots are very tasty, and the reason they are so tasty is because of the Moon – without it, the vegetables wouldn't grow. So, the next time you look at the Moon you can think of this interesting fact.

Chapter Four

Let the process of Bhakti yoga work on you

We will naturally feel like serving Krishna (God), especially after we've tasted Prasadam, food offered to God. By following the simple procedures in this book, love will awaken in our hearts. By letting this process work on us, by following the Bhakti yoga way of gardening, we will realise that plants are valuable beings; indeed, some plants are even more productive than some humans!

There are many mentions of plants, of gardening and of sowing seeds in Srila Prabhupada's books. Lord Caitanya, the 15th Century avatar of Lord Krishna, considered himself a gardener, one who planted seeds of divine love in the hearts of many. In the Bible Jesus says: "as you sow, so shall you reap". That's an explanation of karma; for every action there is an equal reaction. Hare Krishna devotee Devi Dasi has compiled a book called *Speaking about Varnasrama* wherein Srila Prabhupada encourages devotees to grow their own food, indeed, he considered anything home-grown to be far better than anything bought in a shop. Prabhupada also considered it to be a great act of love if someone gave him something from their garden. Many people give me produce from their gardens, so I can conclude that they have love in their hearts for me. In the Bhagavad-gītā, Chapter 10 text 9, Srila Prabhupada writes in his purport about seeds and plants:

mac-citta mad-gata-prana
bodhayantah parasparam
kathayantas ca mam nityam
tusyanti ca ramanti ca

"The thoughts of my pure devotee's dwell in me, their lives are fully devoted to my service, and they derive great satisfaction and bliss from always enlightening one another and conversing about me".

The reason I mention this verse is because in the purport to this verse Srila Prabhupada writes that Lord Caitanya likens transcendental devotional service to the sowing of a seed in the heart of the living entity. Lord Caitanya is Krishna himself, who appeared in India just over 500 years ago. I recommend the reader of this book to read the version of the Bhagavad-gītā known as *Bhagavada-gītā As It Is*, then *Śrīmad-Bhāgavatam*, then Śrī Caitanya-caritāmṛta. All are written by A.C. Bhaktivedanta swami Prabhupada. Best to read these books in the order I've listed them.

Prabhupada himself liked very much that devotees grow their own food. He travelled the world eleven times between the ages of seventy and eighty, starting farm communities, schools and temples. He loved to sit in the garden.

When the seed is planted in the heart of the living entity, we cultivate the seed by hearing and chanting the Mahā-mantra:

Hare Krishna Hare Krishna Krishna Krishna Hare Hare Hare
Rama Hare Rama Rama Rama Hare Hare

The spiritual plant of devotional service gradually grows until it penetrates the covering of the material universe. When the spiritual plant reaches the spiritual world, it grows until it reaches Goloka Vrindavan, the highest spiritual planet, where Krishna lives. The plant takes shelter at the lotus feet of Krishna, where it produces flowers and fruit. In Goloka Vrindavan the plant becomes fully absorbed in the love of God.

This is a very nice example of how we can relate gardening to practicing spiritual life, and there are many other explanations like this in the books I've listed.

Gardening is a community activity; it is easy to make friends with fellow gardeners. We can share our knowledge, our enthusiasm and our produce with others. If you have a garden you can speak to your neighbours about gardening, or if you have an allotment, you can share your experiences and results with others on the allotment site. I've always found it easy to make friends on allotment sites. It's easy to speak to others on an allotment because of the common interest of growing produce. It is always good to help others that are having any difficulties with gardening.

Chapter Five

Prepare your consciousness for gardening

It is best to be prepared for the spring. Make sure all the pots and trays you are going to use are clean. The easy way to clean pots and trays is to use a small brush with a handle on it, like the kind we use for cleaning pots at home that you can buy from the ironmongers for one or two pounds. Make sure you have all the tools you need, you have bought all the seeds you need, that you have seed compost and potting compost and that you have the ground you're going to grow in prepared and ready for planting.

Any keen gardener will always encourage gardening newcomers; with gardening we can learn new things every day, even up to our nineties. It is good to share tips even with experienced gardeners.

Gardening the Bhakti yoga way means we prepare our consciousness before we start the day's work. If we prepare properly the work can be fun. Preparation starts as early in the morning as possible. We do not only prepare the soil, we prepare our consciousness as well.

The best way to prepare our consciousness is to rise early in the morning, pay obeisances to our spiritual masters and recite the guru-vastika prayers in glorification of our teachers. I'm adding these prayers to this book because I prepare every morning by listening to them. They're very beautiful prayers, it's good to read them every morning:

1/ The spiritual master is receiving benediction from the ocean of mercy. Just as a cloud pours water on a forest fire to extinguish it, so the spiritual master delivers the materially afflicted world by extinguishing the blazing fire of material existence. I offer my respectful obeisance's unto the lotus feet of such a spiritual master, who is an ocean of all auspicious qualities.

2/ Chanting the holy name, dancing in ecstasy, singing, and playing musical instruments, the spiritual master is always gladdened by the sankirtan movement of Lord Caitanya Mahaprabhu. Because he is relishing the mellows of pure devotion within his mind, sometimes his hair stands on end, he feels quivering in his body, and tears flow from his eyes like waves. I offer my respectful obacancies unto the lotus feet of such a spiritual master.

3/ The spiritual master is always engaged in temple worship of Sri Sri Radha and Krishna. He also engages his disciples in such worship. They dress the deities in beautiful clothes and ornaments, clean their temple, and perform similar worship of the lord. I offer my respectful obacancies unto the lotus feet of such a spiritual master.

4/ The spiritual master is always offering Krishna four kinds of delicious food (analysed as that which is licked, chewed, drunk and sucked). When the spiritual master sees that the devotees are satisfied by eating bhagavata-prasada, he is satisfied. I offer my respectful obacancies unto the lotus feet of such a spiritual master.

5/ The spiritual master is always eager to hear and chant about the unlimited conjugal pastimes of Radhika and Madhava, and their qualities names and forms. The spiritual master aspires to relish these at every moment. I offer my respectful obacancies unto the lotus feet of such a spiritual master.

6/ The spiritual master is very dear, because he is expert in assisting the gopis, who at different times make different tasteful arrangements for the perfection of Radha and Krishna's conjugal loving affairs within the groves of Vrindavana. I offer my most humble obacancies unto the lotus feet of such a spiritual master.

7/ The spiritual master is to be honoured as much as the Supreme Lord, because he is the most confidential servitor of the lord. This is acknowledged in all revealed scriptures and followed by all authorities. Therefore, I offer my respectful obacancies unto the lotus feet of such a spiritual master, who is a bonafide representative of Sri Hari (Krishna).

8/ By the mercy of the spiritual master, one receives the benediction of Krishna. Without the grace of the spiritual master, one cannot make any advancement. Therefore, I should always remember and praise the spiritual master, at least three times a day I should offer my respectful obacancies unto the lotus feet of my spiritual master.

It's also nice to listen to kirtan and the Tulasi prayers. Tulsi is a goddess in the form of a plant.

Tulsi prayers

1/ O Tulsi beloved of Krishna, I bow down before you again and again. My desire is to obtain the service of Sri Sri Radha and Krishna.

2/ Whoever takes shelter of you has his wishes fulfilled. Bestowing your mercy on him, you make him a resident of Vrindavan.

3/ My desire is that you will also give me a residence in the pleasure groves of Sri Vrindavana dhama. Thus, within my vision I will always behold the beautiful pastimes of Radha and Krishna.

4/ I beg to you to make me a follower of the cowherd damsels of Vraj. Please give me the privilege of devotional service and make me your own maid servant.

5/ This very fallen and lowly servant of Krishna prays, "May I always swim in the love of Sri Sri Radha and Govinda".

I also listen to the Sri Nrsimha Pranamas for protection:

1/ I offer my obacancies to Lord Nrsimha who gives joy to Prahlada Maharaj and whose nails are like chisels on the stonelike chest of the demon Hiranyakasipu. Lord Nrsimha is here, and he is also there. Wherever I go Lord Nrsimha is there. He is in the heart and outside as well. I surrender to lord Nrsimha, the origin of all things and the supreme refuge.

2/ O Kesava! O lord of the universe! O Lord Hari, who have assumed the form of half man, half lion! All glories to you! Just as one can easily crush a wasp between one's fingernails, so the same way the body of the wasp like demon Hiranyakasipu has been ripped apart by the wonderful, pointed nails on your beautiful lotus hands.

After I listen to those prayers I chant Japa on beads, as many rounds as is practically possible, and chant as attentively as possible. Japa means we chant the Mahā-mantra softly to ourselves so we can hear it, the Mahā-mantra is:

*Hare Krishna Hare Krishna Krishna Krishna Hare Hare Hare
Rama Hare Rama Rama Rama Hare Hare*

It is also good to associate with others by doing devotional activities together during the morning program, that way we will become more enthusiastic. Meditation and prayers can be just as effective at home as they are in a temple.

The secret to chanting is to let the mantra work on you. Sacinandana Swami, an initiating spiritual master in ISKCON, says we should be the receiver not the achiever, do not try to force anything out of the mantra and do not expect sudden enlightenment.

Practice makes perfect, give things time and chant with others if possible. There are many good books on chanting available and many good lectures online by devotees like Mahatma Das. It is also good to have a hearty breakfast, cooked from produce that you have grown yourself and offered to Lord Krishna. I will give easy to follow guidelines on how to offer food to Krishna. We call the food that has been offered to Krishna 'Prasadam', and it is particularly good to respect the Prasadam in a peaceful atmosphere with a nice Krishna Bhajan playing. A good meditation whilst taking Prasadam is that this sanctified food is the whole spiritual world in an edible form, and while taking Prasadam we are taking part in Radha and Krishna's pastimes. Radha is Krishna's spiritual female consort. By serving our spiritual master we are assisting him in making tasteful arrangements for Radha and Krishna's pastimes in the spiritual world. We are serving our spiritual master by taking Prasadam.

We need plenty of energy if we are going to be digging or building a compost heap, so it is very good to eat things like porridge with dried fruit and nuts or bread and kitchari. Kitchari is a type of vegetarian stew made with dhal, rice and vegetables and we should eat to our full satisfaction so that we are happy in the garden. It is always good to invite fellow gardeners for lunch and it is always very nice to harvest the produce with others and prepare the produce for cooking with others. When people are new to gardening it is very good to get them involved in harvesting and preparation, then, after we have offered the produce to Krishna, we can serve it to others and sit and enjoy the meal with those who appreciate the taste and the work that has gone into producing it. It is also good to mention at the meal how kind Krishna is to provide for us.

Chapter Six

Love thy neighbour

You do not need a big garden to be enthusiastic about growing; you can grow on a small window box, or grow tomatoes and peppers on a sunny window ledge. If you have windows that face out onto the street it is good to have window boxes and a hanging basket at the door; for a hanging basket it is good to put trailing plants like Petunia Surfinia, Lobelia and Fuchsia to hang over the sides with marigolds and geraniums at the top. For a window box one metre in length, you can plant three or four trailing petunia plants with marigolds and geraniums, three of each, for the top. If you have a greenhouse, it's best to buy the seedlings in April from a garden centre and then plant them in the middle of April; leave them in your greenhouse or polytunnel, and cover with garden fleece which you can buy very cheaply from the garden centre.

If you do not have a greenhouse, then it is best to not put the window box or hanging basket out until the middle or even the end of May if you live in a cold climate. I have grown an attractive window box in Scotland without a greenhouse, so I know it's possible. Hanging baskets and window boxes are great for creating a good impression with your neighbours and other people on the street. Do not forget that the plants are all devotees! It states in the Bhagavad-gītā that of the seasons, Krishna is the flower bearing spring. If your neighbours and friends appreciate that you have made the world more beautiful by creating a nice flower display, then that's great! The flowers I mentioned are not especially fragrant but there are some particularly fragrant flowers, such as hyacinths, that you can buy as bulbs and then plant in well-drained soil; plant them twice the depth of the bulb. If the soil is not well-drained, you can add a bit of horticultural sand. You can grow hyacinths in a few pots at the doorway or under the window, or in a rockery or a small part of your front garden if you have one. Hyacinths grow in the spring along with daffodils. Tulips also give colour in spring, and you can plant them just like hyacinths. Krishna is the flower bearing spring, so spring is a very beautiful time of year and if we see beautiful flower displays in the spring then we can appreciate Krishna by seeing the beauty of spring as Krishna's creation. Plant the hyacinths or tulips in October and they will come up at the end of February, March or April of the following year. It is always nice to grow flowers to decorate a small altar at home. It is easy to make garlands with marigolds or hyacinths. Night scented stock is also nice and is easy to grow in the back garden; it has a heavenly fragrance so, if you are sitting in the garden in the evening, it's not only a beautiful sight but you can also enjoy its lovely aroma. You can also plant daffodil bulbs in October and pick them in February the following year to decorate your altar with. It is nice to grow flowers that you can pick throughout the summer. Bulbs generally need to be planted about six months before they flower, so if you plant correctly in advance you can enjoy daffodils in February, then hyacinths in March, April and May, and then marigolds in June and July. Sow marigold seeds in March, then gladioli in August, September and October – if you plant gladioli bulbs in October you can have flowers for garlands and for displays all spring and summer.

You can also grow carnations in the summer. For hanging baskets and window boxes it is easy to buy compost from the garden centres and it is even possible to make your own compost with old plants from the garden, as well as from vegetable and fruit peelings, but do not put cooked food in the compost heap because it may attract rats. If there are worms in your compost heap do not put citrus fruit in. I will write more about compost later in this book. You can grow flowers all year round if you have a heated greenhouse.

Even if you just have a small house with a small garden or you can only make a small display at the front, it can make such a positive difference in your life. Gardening the Bhakti yoga way can make you feel positive, enthusiastic and happy, and you can improve the local area with a flower display. The more that people do a flower display in their homes, the more beautiful the word will become. You can make a difference. One drop of snow doesn't seem to make a difference when it's snowing but after a few hours of snow the whole ground is white, similarly, every small effort we make to please Krishna purifies our hearts and eventually we become completely pure, so if we are making an effort to put a nice flower display outside our home to create a good impression with our neighbours, Krishna is pleased with that as much as when we share our meals of Prasadam with our neighbours and friends. In that way Krishna will be happy and Mother Bhumi (mother earth) will be pleased, after all Bhakti yoga is all about pleasing the devotees and pleasing Krishna. Everyone is a devotee, so it is nice to please as many people as possible. During the last year I was in my back garden a lot due to the Covid-19 lockdown and my neighbours were also in their back garden, so we were swapping tools, plants and foodstuff. My neighbours, Sylvia and Levi, really liked my pizza. I couldn't get out to the garden centre this year to get flowers and my marigolds died because of a bad frost in mid-May so I couldn't do a flower display at the front of our house, so in the beginning of July, my wife Palika Devi came in one Sunday morning and told me there was a surprise for me outside. I walked out of the front door and our neighbour Sylvia had planted our front plant boxes up with small colourful begonias. Sylvia has set a great example of what it means to love thy neighbour.

Your garden can look very attractive and at the same time be very productive. If you plant rainbow chard and Swiss chard with beetroot, red cabbage, cauliflowers and green cabbage, you can have lots of different colours; you could even plant strawberries and have a border of flowers like marigolds and some other colourful flowers of your choice like dwarf cornflowers. I got this idea from Jeff Hamilton, one of my gardening gurus. I watched a program he made, called 'The Ornamental Kitchen Garden', and I found it so inspiring. An ornamental kitchen garden can look very attractive all summer and produce all season. If you want to produce fruit, vegetables and flowers and you also want your garden to look good, you could do a small ornamental kitchen garden just for fun. It's great to be creative when gardening, an ornamental kitchen garden can look beautiful and create a good mood for those who visit it.

Gardening can be very therapeutic, especially when we

connect it to Krishna. Gardening done with love is very good therapy; 'all you need is love', is a song by a very famous group of musicians and if we garden with love then we can solve all of our problems. The idea is to grow fruits, vegetables and flowers and offer them to Krishna. In that way we cultivate love for Krishna in our hearts. If we want to love others it's a good idea to start by loving ourselves as souls, and if we are growing fruits, vegetables and flowers then we can have love for ourselves because we are properly connected to Krishna. If we love ourselves because we're Krishna's then it won't be long before we are back in the spiritual world where we will be eternally happy and live forever, free from all suffering. When picking flowers, vegetables or fruits from your ornamental garden, choose carefully what you're picking so that the garden stays attractive throughout the season. If you manage it properly it should be able to supply you with nice fruit and vegetables for cooking and offering as well as flowers for displays throughout the whole season, and your garden will still be very beautiful.

Chapter Seven

Community gardens

There are many community gardens, and you can find them in most small towns and cities. If there is no community garden in your local area, then my advice is to start one yourself. Community gardens are great places to make new friends and good contacts. I once popped into Woodlands Community Garden in Glasgow and had a chat with the organiser who then showed me around; I left my email and a few weeks later I was invited to their open day, during which a very enthusiastic woman named Eco Mackenzie gave an incredible talk on the subject of growing organic fruit and vegetables. Eco supplied some of the top hotels in Glasgow with organic fruit and vegetables.

I sat down and spoke with Eco while we were having lunch after her talk. I told her what I was doing at the Krishna Eco Farm in Lesmahagow and invited her to the farm. She visited us a few weeks later and loved the project where I had been growing produce for twenty years. Two weeks later, myself and some of our volunteers went up to Eco's farm and had a nice lunch from her garden. Eco showed us around and recommended us to some of her volunteers who then came and stayed with us and did some work. We also recommended Eco's place to some of our own volunteers. She used to come down to our place with a few of her volunteers on a Sunday for the famous Hare Krishna Sunday love feast. A few of Eco's volunteers stayed with us for a couple of weeks and helped us with our gardening project.

While living in a small town called Stonehouse in South Lanarkshire, I took part in the Brighter Village project. A group of local people got together and planted bulbs around the village. They arranged wooden plant boxes and placed them around – this is a great way to get to know local people if you're new in town. If one is unemployed or at home and on their own, it is good to get out and about and meet local people. On more than one occasion, my voluntary work has led me to full time paid work. One can find lots of community gardens just by a simple Google search, or you can inquire with your local council.

One day a group from the Stonehouse Brighter Village project turned up at the Krishna Eco Farm in Lesmahagow. I was surprised! I hadn't seen them for some years although I had invited them while I was volunteering for their organisation. I showed them around and they were happy with their experience at the Krishna Eco Farm. I served them some Prasadam made with fruit and vegetables from our farm.

Gardening can be incredibly good for one's mental health; it is a very sociable activity and when we see plants grow, we become very enthusiastic and inspired. Harvesting the produce can make one incredibly positive. It is genuinely nice to prepare the fruit and vegetables for a meal with others. I love picking tomatoes, lettuce and cucumbers with new volunteers and preparing them, offering them to Krishna, and then serving them to others. It is great sitting together and listening to everyone commenting on how nice the salad from the garden is.

I once volunteered at a horticultural therapy project in Edinburgh called Redhall Walled Garden, which was a very well organised project. They had a five-day working week, each day beginning at nine in the morning and going until four in the afternoon, with one hour for lunch. People who attended the project benefited from the regulated working day and the staff were very supportive. The trainees harvested the produce from the garden, prepared and cooked it, and everyone took the meal together at lunchtime. This project was very good for people who were unemployed or having difficulty with mental health issues such as depression or anxiety. Some people just wanted to get out of their house or flat, meet people and learn some gardening. Jan, the manager of the project, recommended me to the Botanic Garden in Edinburgh where I did some training on their herbaceous border. She also introduced me to Acme Organics, a small walled garden near Peebles in Scotland where I helped to grow fruit and vegetables. Zeb and Claire, who owned Acme Organics, were very hospitable. Jan also introduced me to Wiston Lodge, an old hunting lodge at the foot of a famous hill called Tinto. Wiston Lodge is no longer a hunting lodge, it is used to give youths from the inner cities a break in the country. My job at Wiston Lodge was to look after the kitchen garden and supply the kitchen with fresh fruit and vegetables. I made many friends at Wiston.

The staff at the Redhall horticultural project were happy with me because I treated the trainees with respect and made friends with them. I saw many of the trainees at Redhall benefit from growing flowers, fruit and vegetables. One of the reasons I am writing this book is to help to revive the vegetable growing culture in the world and to make the world a more beautiful place, as well as to help improve people's attitude toward one another.

I am still friends with many of the trainees who attended Redhall and many members of the staff there have continued to help me with my personal relationships as well with as my gardening career.

I've gone a lot more into detail about horticultural therapy later in this book, mainly because it has helped me so much. I'm an insignificant soul, who's dependent on the devotees and Krishna. I've tried to stress how much the people involved and Krishna have helped me.

I would be delighted to see more and more community gardens springing up all over the world. One project in Glasgow called the Coach House Trust did such a good job of beautifying a derelict site between some buildings. Poppy, the gardening instructor there, was such a caring person and she will live forever in my heart.

I live in Lesmahagow, a small town not far from Lanark, just off the M74 and 30 miles south of Glasgow. There is a lot of nice countryside around Lesmahagow and so I often go out for a walk. One Sunday morning I decided to go for a walk and pop into a place called Talhm Life community. It's about three miles from Lesmahagow so it was a nice place for a rest. I just thought I would pop in to say hello and to see if there was a way we could perhaps work together. I met Stevi after walking around for a few minutes. He was very friendly and introduced me to some of the volunteers he was working with. Stevi and I immediately struck up a friendship that has lasted to this day, fifteen years later. Stevi took me to an orchard in the Clyde Valley, which was owned by Jeremy, a friend of his. What a beautiful orchard it is! The Clyde Valley is famous for orchards; Clyde Valley tomatoes were famous back when I was a boy. Jeremy's orchard has two hundred plum trees and twenty apple trees, as well as a few pear trees.

Jeremy gave me a piece of land to work with, so I grew some potatoes there. I made a deal with Jeremy; myself and the volunteers from the Krishna Eco Farm would do the work to maintain the orchard and in return we would get as much fruit as we liked. We had a good time working in the orchard and picking fruit and I will never forget sitting in Jeremy's caravan having lunch one day with Phil, Berta and a few other volunteers. It was amazing to see how absorbed in the Prasadam Phil was. Phil and Berta now live in Spain. They grow food, cook it and offer it to Krishna, and they travel around in their mobile restaurant selling the food which they have produced. I'm proud of them and happy to have played a part in their success. Many devotees at the eco farm have enjoyed the apple and pear crumbles that came from the orchard – the fruit juice from the blackcurrants that came from it was like nectar. We used to put the fruit from the orchard in our porridge at the Krishna Eco Farm in the morning. So, it was a worthwhile walk all those years ago and I'm so glad that I visited Talhm that day.

I had a life changing experience involving the same orchard. I have a good friend named Jayadeva. He's a musician, teaches meditation and yoga and he does very nice therapies. I went to visit him one day and while we were talking, he put on some nice music, a track by his daughter Gaurangi called 'come out of the darkness and into the light'. I loved the whole experience of being able to open up with him and to be myself since Jayadeva is such a friendly person and the music was so beautiful. I was able to enter into a nice meditation about being in the orchard with some family members and friends and my life changed as a result of that meditation. I came out of Jayadeva's house feeling a lot lighter than when I went in; a heavy burden which had been weighing me down for a long time had lifted. I'm eternally indebted to Stevi and to Jayadeva.

Working with WWOOF volunteers

WWOOF means 'worldwide opportunities on organic farms'. There are many people of all ages who are enthusiastic to work on organic farms so that they can get the experience of living and working in such an environment. The WWOOF host simply has to provide bed and board for the volunteer. I've worked with WWOOF volunteers on a few farms, mainly the Krishna Eco Farm in Lesmahagow. Young and enthusiastic volunteers always bring a lot of life to any project they are working on. Growing organic fruit, vegetables and flowers is especially fun when working with other people who are enthusiastic to be there.

While growing produce the Bhakti yoga way, I've worked with people who don't believe in God, but they still make spiritual advancement because they are following my lead and I am following the prescribed process of Bhakti yoga which was taught to me by my teacher, who was taught by his teacher, and that line of teachers goes all the way back to Krishna Himself. Working with people from all around the world broadens the mind and the great thing about gardening with others is that we can talk things over and have discussions while weeding or picking fruit. I've made lots of friends working on organic farms. The WWOOF volunteers have been a big plus to my life.

A nice allotment story

While we were visiting friends in Somerset, myself and my wife, Palika Devi, went to a place called Frome one Sunday. We were in the town centre distributing devotional books. A lot of the shops were closed and there weren't many people around, but the people who were around and who I spoke to were very nice; they took books and gave some money. It was a nice sunny day, so we decided to go for a walk along the riverbank. A river runs through the centre of Frome and so we walked along the bank and after about ten minutes we came to some allotments. Palika suggested that we go for a walk around the site, so we walked around the paths in the allotments and said hello to the people who were there. I kept some of Srila Prabhupada's books in my hand as we were walking around, and we passed an allotment where a lady was working. She asked me what books I had in my hand, and I told her that I had *Higher Taste* and *Chant and be Happy*, so she said "I'll take those two books", and she gave me five pounds. She said she had read the *Bhagavad-gītā As It Is* by Srila Prabhupada. She was a Christian and I told her that she had shown us the true spirit of love of God. The test for someone who is practising any religion is if they are cultivating love of God, it doesn't matter what religion they are following, the test is: are they making spiritual advancement? This lady was a Christian, but she was happy to read our books and show love towards us. I could see that she must be making tangible spiritual advancement in her life. So, we never know what's going to happen if we get out and about, meet people and speak with them. I'm always surprised at how nice people are when I speak to them about spiritual life.

Some people that I really don't expect to take to spiritual life end up surprising me. I was in my hometown of Coatbridge in Scotland recently and the people there were very nice. A spiritual exchange might seem like an insignificant exchange to some, but the fact is that the love exchanged in a spiritual interaction will change the world for the better to some extent. If a lot of people do a little, then the world will change for the better.

*Spring at the Krishna eco farm
Lesmahagow, Scotland*

Very nice hanging baskets

My little paradise

Salad from the garden

My window ledge in spring

Walking in our favourite rose garden

Plums freshly picked from the orchard in the Clyde valley, Scotland

I love walking in this garden with friends

Veggie soup made from veg from my garden

Raspberry jam

Ardengraig garden Rothesay

The botanical gardens Edinburgh

*Radha and Krishna nicely
decorated with flowers*

Chapter Eight

Gardening with Love and Devotion for Lord Krishna

Here I will explain how we can relate to Krishna (God) while we are in the garden.

Plants also have souls. The difference between a human and a plant is the bodily difference, the soul in the plant is the same in quality as the soul in the human being. We can engage the plants in devotional service, Bhakti yoga, by offering the fruit, flowers and vegetables to Krishna.

In the Bhagavad-gītā, chapter 9 text 26 Krishna says:

> *patraṁ puṣpaṁ phalaṁ toyaṁ*
> *yo me bhaktyā*
> *prayacchati tad ahaṁ*
> *bhakty-upahṛtam aśnāmi*
> *prayatātmanaḥ*

'If one offers me with love and devotion a leaf, a flower, a fruit or water, I will accept it'.

Also, in a book called *Speaking about Varnasrama*, Srila Prabhupada says that home grown produce is a hundred times better than that bought in a shop. Once when someone brought some fruit and vegetables from his garden and gave them as a gift to Prabhupada, Prabhupada said that it is real love to give someone fruit and vegetables from your garden.

Prabhupada very much wanted devotees to organise farms and to live off the land, growing as much of their own produce as possible. In all my years of gardening, many people have given me produce from their gardens and that is to their eternal benefit, since I always offer any produce anyone has given me from their garden to Krishna and I share it with as many people as I can.

In a very advanced spiritual book about the pastimes of Lord Caitanya Mahaprabhu called *Śrī Caitanya-caritāmṛta*, Lord Caitanya, who is Krishna himself, is described as a gardener who sows the seeds of love of God in the hearts of souls.

So, God considers Himself to be a gardener. This is because when we are practising love of God, it is understood that we are cultivating a creeper of devotion in our hearts, therefore we take care to cultivate the seed and creeper of devotion by watering it with devotional service and we uproot the weeds of material desires. So, we can compare cultivating devotional service to gardening, keeping in mind that every individual plant is a devotee. If we use the produce from the fruit tree by offering it to Krishna, then the tree will take a human body in its next life or even go back to Godhead. We can also water the plants with Caritamarta, or holy water.

If you do add Krishna to your life by offering the produce from your garden to Him, you will notice improvements in your consciousness. If you already offer the produce from your garden to Krishna, then don't stop doing that. If you don't grow any fruit, veg or flowers, then now is a good time to start. If you make a move towards Krishna, he will work wonders in your life. I was living ten miles from a garden which I trained at in

Edinburgh. One morning my landlord, Paul, came round to visit me. He said that he had a flat to rent in another part of Edinburgh and so I went to look at the flat. It was near the garden I was training in and so I took it. I could see that Krishna had made that arrangement.

After I'd been training at that garden for a while, a woman called Linda came in one morning and asked if anyone wanted a job doing her garden. I took the job and made friends with Linda who I invited, along with her friends, to the Krishna Eco Farm in Lesmahagow. They accepted my invitation and visited the project. I also invited to the farm many people I trained with and with whom I worked. All the people I worked for gave me good references. I gave the references to our temple president, Prabhupada Prana, and he gave the references to the government. As a result, we got a grant.

Not only did I learn how to grow fruit, vegetables and flowers properly, but I also made lots of friends. So, by adding Krishna to our life, we can improve our personal relationships.

Chapter Nine

How to grow

Cold frame

Seedlings must be accustomed to outside temperatures if grown in a heated greenhouse or propagator. A cold frame is quite easy to build. Just make a wooden or brick rectangle structure about two feet high and two yards long, it can be smaller if you only have a few seed trays. Make a wooden frame the same size as the rectangle and cover it with clear plastic or cover the structure with old windows. You can put hinges on the lid or just lift it off. Use materials that are lying around if possible as that will save money and it's fun looking for things that have been discarded, such as old pallets, old furniture or old bricks. Make sure the structure is safe, especially if there are going to be kids around. Place your seedlings in the cold frame and keep them watered. Plants can stay in the cold frame for one to four weeks.

Apples

It's always nice to have an apple tree in the garden. You don't need so much room since there are dwarf varieties. Apples aren't so difficult to grow, although they don't grow so well on the coast where there are salt laden winds, and in the north there may be a problem with frost, although I've grown many apple trees in Scotland which have produced lots of apples. Just be careful what varieties you choose.

Apple trees grow best in a sunny, sheltered site. They will

grow well in most soils, but you should avoid waterlogged ground or soil with a high lime content when choosing a site to plant. The ideal soil is a slightly acidic type that does not dry out in the summer. Prepare the site where the trees are to grow in late September or early October. Fork in well-rotted manure or compost, one bucket per square metre. When choosing trees, buy two in the same pollination group, for example Discovery and Merton have blossom at about the same time and will cross-pollinate. It is also possible to buy family trees in which three or four varieties are grafted on a single rootstock to provide a succession of fruit.

The best time to plant fruit trees is during frost-free weather between early November and late March. Dig a hole of sufficient size to take the roots when they are well spread out, hammer in a supporting stake and plant the tree close against it. Make sure that the union between the stock and the scion is at least 4 inches (100 mm) above soil level. Water well during dry periods in the first season and mulch around the trees with compost or soil for the first few springs.

Training and pruning. During the first four years of a tree's life, the aim should be to create a strong framework of branches. It may be better to buy a tree that has been partially trained by the nurseryman. A tip for pruning is the three ds: dead-damaged-diseased. Always prune at an angle so the water doesn't sit on the surface of the pruned branch. Burn dead, damaged and diseased branches and don't let branches rub against each other, that will cause disease. After planting a two-year-old bush tree, shorten the branch leaders by about half to two-thirds so that the tips of the branches are roughly level. Prune to an outward facing bud – the following summer a number of lateral shoots will have to grow from the branches. In the next winter, choose some of these to form more branches; these should all point upwards and outwards. As a general rule, prune them back to an outward facing bud. The branches of some varieties, however, have a slightly drooping habit, and these are sometimes pruned back to an inward facing bud. Shorten new growth by one third if it is vigorous, and by half if it is weaker.

After pruning, the tips of the branch leaders should be at least 18in (455mm) from their nearest neighbour and more or less level with each other. Laterals not chosen to form main branches should be cut back to four buds from the base to form future fruiting spurs. Laterals crowding the centre can either be shortened or removed. This pruning establishes the basic shape of the tree, although it may be necessary to carry out a little more formative pruning for the next two or three years. Subsequent pruning of a bush tree depends on whether it is a spur bearer or a tip bearer. A tip bearer bears fruit both on the spurs and at the tips of the shoots, the proportion differing with each variety.

Pruning an over vigorous tree. If a tree has grown too tall, cut it back gradually over three or four winters to reduce the shock of severe pruning. Cut out branches to open up the centre of the tree and reduce the height of others to make fruit picking easier.

First cut back high branches in the centre to the main trunk. Prune back outer, tall-growing branches to a lower branch. Lightly thin out smaller laterals and young growth. After four years the main branches should be well spaced out. Start to thin the crop in early June if the crop is very heavy; I've seen branches break due to too much fruit on the branch. There will be a natural drop but that may not be enough, at the same time don't take too much fruit off the tree. Apples should be about 4–6in (9100–230mm) apart, large cooking apples a bit more, but don't worry if the tree is too high or too thin, it should still produce plenty of apples. To store them, just check that the apples are not damaged and wrap them in paper. Store in a cool room. Happy apple picking and remember to add berries if you're making an apple crumble.

Artichokes

Artichokes like a warm sunny spot and they grow well in free-draining soil. Dig in some well-rotted manure the winter before you plan to grow and add some compost before you plant. You can grow artichokes from seed. Sow in March or April, 13mm (½in) deep, or buy small plants from a garden centre. Plant them 60–90cm deep and 2–3ft apart in a permanent position in May. Artichoke plants will produce about five or six heads and will continue to produce for four to six years. It's best to remove the buds in the first year so that the plants produce larger heads the second year. You can propagate plants by dividing clumps to produce more plants. Don't forget to weed and water during dry spells. In cold areas, cut the main stem down to almost ground level and cover the plants in late autumn with compost or straw to protect them from frost. In the spring, feed them with well-rotted manure or compost. In the second and third years allow each plant four to six stems. Leave the flower on the main stem and several others at the end of the lateral shoots; nip off any extra buds on the side shoots. Plants should be ready for harvest in June or July. Pick the king headfirst when it is green and tightly wrapped. The heads on the lateral shoots are best when they are about the size of a hen's egg.

Asparagus

Asparagus is a perennial plant which needs shelter from the wind. It grows well in rich, well-drained soil. Dig a bed in autumn 4ft (½m) wide and plant two rows in that bed. Dig well-rotted manure or compost into the topsoil, a bucketful per square yard. Asparagus can be grown from seed, or you can buy plants which are one year old. Plant during April in England and May in Scotland. Dig trenches 8in (200mm) deep, 3ft (1m) apart. Make sure the trenches are wide enough to plant roots when spread out. Replace 2in (50mm) of soil. Plant the asparagus 18 inches (455mm) apart in the trenches. Spread out the roots and cover quickly with soil. Cover the trenches with 3in (75mm) of soil and firm the surface. Gradually draw soil from the sides, by October the soil should be level. Cut the ferns down in November, when yellow, to 1in (25mm) above the soil and mulch with compost. Don't harvest shoots grown from one year's crowns during the first two seasons. Take only one or two spears from each plant in the third year. After the third year, harvest for only six weeks. Allow shoots to grow into ferns. Plants should produce for twenty years if grown this way. Harvest the shoots when they are about 4in (100mm) above the soil. Cut the spears 4in (100mm) below the soil.

Basil

Basil is a herb that goes well with tomatoes in salad. There are two types of basil: sweet basil and bush basil. It's best to grow basil in a polytunnel or a greenhouse if the weather isn't so warm; basil can be grown outside in a warm climate. Sweet Basil grows to a height of 2–3ft (610mm). Bush basil grows to a height of 6–12 in (150–305mm).

Sow the seeds in March in a tray and put on a sunny window ledge or into a propagator. Transfer into 5in (130mm) pots when they are large enough to handle. Basil can also be grown outside if the weather is good. Sow the seeds in a warm sheltered site in well-drained fertile soil in drills ¼in (5mm) deep. Thin out the seedlings to 12in (305mm) apart. Be sure to keep the plants well-watered, especially if they are in a greenhouse or a polytunnel. Pinch out the flower buds to encourage the leaves to grow. Pick when required.

Beetroot

I love growing beetroots because they taste so good, and I like to slowly roast them in the oven. Grow beetroot on a sunny site in sandy soil or add a bit of sand if the soil is heavy. Do not use manure on soil where you are growing beetroot, use compost instead. I grow different varieties like Boltardy, Golden ball, and Detroit. Sow seeds from March to June, or June to July if you are in the north. Sow the seeds in drills ¾in (20mm) deep, 12in (305mm) apart and scatter the seeds along the drills about 1in (25mm) apart. You can thin the beetroots when they are about half the size of a golf ball, they are edible at that size. After thinning, the beetroots should be about 4in (100mm) apart. Do not grow over cricket ball size or the beetroots will become woody and lose their flavour. Harvest when needed. Store in boxes of sand after cutting off the leaves 1in (25mm) from the beetroot.

Blackcurrants

My favourite soft fruit to grow because it is so easy to grow and propagate, and the plants also produce lots of fruit. Blackcurrants are richer in vitamin C than most garden fruits. It's best to plant and grow blackcurrants in a sunny situation although they will grow in partial shade. Plant blackcurrant plants in well-draining soil that has been well manured. There are many varieties of blackcurrant bushes to choose from, so always check which varieties are good for your area by speaking to a local grower. Varieties include Boskoop Giant, Baldwin late and Malling jet.

It's best to buy certified disease-free plants from a nursery and plant in the autumn or throughout winter as long as the soil is not frozen. Plant the bushes 5–6ft (1.5–1.8m) apart. There will be a soil mark on the plant, so plant a little deeper than they were planted in the nursery. After planting, prune all the shoots to about 1in (25mm) above ground level, cutting just above a bud. This means that the bushes will yield no fruit the first summer, instead their energy will be used to produce vigorous new growth. After pruning, mulch the plants with a layer of compost or manure and repeat the mulching every spring at a rate of two buckets per square yard or metre in order to feed and conserve the soil. Be careful not to disturb the roots while weeding and to water the plants during dry spells. Every autumn, remove some of the older wood to make way for replacement shoots, cut low down to promote new growth from near ground level and if you have old bushes which have been a bit neglected then cut out the old wood from the centre to let the air and light in. The old wood, which will be darker, requires hard pruning to stimulate new growth. Do not go crazy pruning, be careful not to prune too many branches or you may kill a plant.

My favourite thing about blackcurrant bushes is that they are easy to propagate. November is a good time to propagate them, just cut a healthy-looking branch near the base, just above a bud, cut it with a slant so that the rain runs off the remaining shoot, and take the branch, which can be from 8inches (200mm) to 2 feet (600mm) long, and plant it in well dug, rich soil with the slant cut end pushed about 6in (150mm) into the soil. By the following spring, your plants should have rooted and be producing some small leaves. You can then carefully transplant the plants, if necessary, by digging up with a fork. Pick blackcurrants a few weeks after they have turned black. Happy planting and picking, and do not forget to share with your friends.

Broad beans

I have grown broad beans many times since they are so easy to grow. Broad beans grow well in rich, well-drained soil; your soil does not have to be in such good condition to grow broad beans, just dig in well-rotted manure the winter before you plant the beans, but do not go overboard with the manure, one bucket per square yard is enough. I generally grow Aguadulce, though there are many varieties to choose from. Make a drill 3in (75mm) deep and sow seeds 6in (150mm) apart, with 9in

(230mm) between the rows. It is best not to grow broad beans on a windy site; you can protect from wind with a windbreak bought from a garden centre, or you can put stakes in the ground at the end of your rows and tie them up with strong string. Pick broad beans before the pods get too hard, it usually takes twelve to fifteen weeks to get from sowing to picking.

Broccoli

I love growing broccoli, especially calabrese, as it is so easy to grow. Like most vegetables, sprouting broccoli is good for a winter crop. Grow broccoli in a sunny situation and sow in seed trays just the same as you would cabbage. Dig in well-rotted manure and compost the autumn or winter before you plant and do not forget to sprinkle some lime on the soil too. Sow calabrese in March and sprouting broccoli in April, or a bit later in a cold climate. Don't forget to use the cold frame if you sow seeds indoors. Sow in drills ½in (12mm) deep in a seed bed and allow 12in (305mm) between rows. Thin the seedlings to 2in (50mm) apart when they have four good leaves. When the plants are about 6in (150mm) tall transplant them into their permanent bed. Plant broccoli 2ft (610mm) apart with 2½ft (760mm) between rows. Sprouting broccoli may be rocked by the wind so drive stakes in to support them when they are 12in (305mm) tall; canes will do, attach them to the canes with string or green gardening wire. Put mats around the bases of the plants to stop cabbage root fly and cover them with nets to stop pigeons from eating them. Cut the heads off the calabrese and let side shoots grow from the stem. When harvesting sprouting broccoli, cut about 4–6in (100–150mm) of the stem and cook with the heads, cut back to a point just above a pair of side shoots which will then produce fresh spears. Harvest calabrese in summer or autumn and sprouting broccoli in the winter.

Brussel sprouts

Brussel sprouts are rich in vitamin C and will provide a crop in autumn and winter. You should grow Brussel sprouts in a sunny situation; dig soil in November to December, add well-rotted manure, compost and lime and sow the seeds during mid-March in ½in (12mm) deep drills, 9in (230mm) apart. Thin the seedlings to 2in (50mm) apart when they are 1in (925mm) high. If the weather is not good or if you live in a cold climate, then sow the seeds in April or May. Don't forget to accustom your plants to outside temperature by putting them in a cold frame before planting them out. You can sow in seed trays just the same way as you sow cabbages. When the plants are about 6in (150mm) tall (around six weeks old), transplant them into their final bed, firm in after transplanting and make sure the plants are 18in (455mm) apart. Put mats around the base of the plants, and cover with nets. Pick the lower sprouts first; sprouts at the top of the plant will swell if you cut the top off the plant, you can cook the top of the plant too. Sprouts are good with applesauce.

Cabbage

There are many different varieties of cabbages including summer cabbage, winter cabbage and spring cabbage. I like to grow Golden acre or Greyhound, and, in the winter, I like Drumhead or January King.

Grow cabbages in a sunny situation in well-drained alkaline soil; dig in some well-rotted manure and add some compost during the previous winter. You can also add some lime; directions will be on the packet regarding how much lime to spread.

Sow seeds in early April for summer cabbages, May for winter cabbages and in July to August for spring cabbages. Sow in a seed tray or outside directly into the soil. I like to sow in a seed tray which has separate compartments, however a normal seed tray will do just fine. Fill the tray with seed compost and pat down firmly, leaving an inch at the top for soil to cover the seeds, or fill separate compartments and put one seed in each compartment. If you are using a normal seed tray, then sprinkle 20 seeds and cover with a thin layer of very fine seed compost, water with a fine rose watering can and put the trays in a propagator or on a sunny window ledge. When seeds have four leaves then transplant them into small pots and after four weeks it's time to plant them outside. Handle the leaves when transplanting and gently remove the plants from the soil, making sure you have some good roots. Firm in after transplanting. If the weather is good where you live you can sow directly outside; but make sure the soil has a fine tilth. Sow in drills ¼in (6mm) deep, then cover with a thin layer of very fine soil, breadcrumb soil I call it. Transplant the seedlings to 2in apart when they have four leaves, then after one month transplant them to 18in (455mm) apart into a permanent bed. It is especially important to sow spring cabbages at the right time so that they survive the winter. Pick cabbages when needed. It is good to grow summer, winter and spring cabbages so that you have a good supply for most of the year. You can put mats, 2in (40mm) square, around the cabbage stem, a square piece of card will do with a cut in it, this will stop cabbage root flies. I always put mats around the base of my cabbages, and I always cover my plants with nets, so the pigeons do not eat them. I have seen pigeons watching me plant cabbages and then waiting for me to go away so that they can eat them. Pigeons will leave you with no cabbages at all if you are not careful.

Carrots

I love growing carrots. I make sweets with carrots, and I also like them with rice and other vegetables. Carrots are easy to grow; grow them in well-drained soil which has not been manured. Add some horticultural sand if you have clay soil. I grow carrots in tubs over two feet high, so that the carrot flies do not get them. There are many varieties: Nantes, Pioneer, Scarlet Perfection, to name but a few. Sow carrots in drills ¼in (5mm) deep in a sunny situation during March, April and May; sow them under cloches if the weather is not so good.

You can thin the seedlings when they get to a few inches high. Thinning should be done on dull days or in the evening since the sun brings out the smell of the carrots and attracts the carrot flies. Harvest them about three months after sowing and there is no harm in eating the odd small carrot raw. If you are growing carrots at ground level, you can cover them with horticultural fleece. You can store carrots in boxes of sand.

Cauliflowers

Cauliflowers can be difficult to grow; they need rich soil and must be kept growing quickly, a spell of drought or a check in growth can result in failure. Dig the plot over the winter before planting and add compost or manure to the soil, one bucket of manure per square yard and add a sprinkle of lime. To grow cauliflowers, sow the seeds in March, April or May and prepare the seed bed in a sunny situation. Sow the seeds in drills ¼in (5mm) deep and space the drills 12in (305mm) apart. Keep the seed bed moist and thin the seedlings when they have four leaves, mature plants need to be 2ft (610mm) apart.

You can start to grow cauliflowers indoors or in a green-house or on a sunny window ledge. Sow the seeds in a seed tray, about 15 seeds per tray. Fill the tray with seed compost almost to the top, pat down the compost firmly and sprinkle seeds on the top, cover with a fine layer of seed compost and water with a light rose watering can. Transplant to small pots when the seedlings have four leaves. After four weeks in small pots, trans-plant the small plants outside to a permanent situation, and put a mat at the base of each plant to stop cabbage root fly and cover with nets. Winter cauliflowers can be grown if you sow all year-round seeds at the end of May.

Coriander

Coriander leaves are good in salad, and Coriander is the easiest herb I have ever grown. It can be grown in a window box out-side or even in a small pot inside. Just sow the coriander seeds by scattering on top of the soil and covering the seeds with a quarter of an inch of soil with a consistency like breadcrumbs. Water with a fine rose watering can and keep watered. Corian-der will grow very quickly, and you could be harvesting it as soon as six weeks after sowing. It will grow in a polytunnel or a greenhouse or even outside if the weather is reasonably good. Plant it in a sunny position. Coriander grows best in well-drained soil which has been enriched with well-rotted manure or compost. Plants grow to about 18in high (455mm) and the seeds can be used to spice food if crushed with a pestle and mortar.

Corn salad

Corn salad can be started in a seed tray indoors in much the same way as lettuce and then transplanted. Grow corn salad in a sunny situation, in well-drained soil containing a generous amount of well-rotted manure or compost. Large leaf Italian is a variety I would recommend. Grow it by sowing in March, April, August and September. Fresh supplies may be grown all year round. For a winter crop sow during August and September. Sow seeds in drills ½in deep (12mm) with 9in (230mm) between rows. Thin the seedlings to 6in (150mm) spacings. Keep the ground well-watered in the first few weeks.

Cucumbers

I love picking cucumbers, chopping them up and adding them to a salad. Fresh cucumbers are delicious, they taste so fresh and really go well with tomatoes and lettuce.

Sow cucumbers during April or May in small pots filled with seed compost. Fill the pots to about 1in from the top and with your finger firmly press the compost down in the pot. Place the seeds in the compost sideways then cover with half an inch of compost, water well using a watering can with a fine shower rose and place the pot on a sunny window ledge or in a propagator. Cucumbers can be grown on a wide window ledge that has high windows, or in a polytunnel or greenhouse. I've built my own small polytunnel (greenhouse) out of spare wood and clear plastic. It's good fun building small structures using materials that are lying around. Some cucumbers can be grown outside if the weather is good, though it may not be a good idea to grow cucumbers outside in a cold climate.

Growing cucumbers indoors. Transfer young plants to 10in (25cm) pots when the plant is about six to eight weeks old and has four strong leaves. Transfer them by gently prizing out the roots and handling the plant by the leaves. If you break the stem then the plant will die but if you slightly damage the leaves the plant will survive, remember the plant is a living being too. Use good potting compost, I will give details of how to make your own compost later. Keep the compost evenly moist, best to water a little as often as possible. Train the main stem up a vertical wire or cane. Pinch out the growing point when the plant reaches the roof, pinch out the tips of the side shoots two leaves beyond a female flower (recognisable by the fruit behind the flower). Pinch out the tips of flowerless side shoots once they reach 60cm (2ft) long.

Cucumbers grow best in humid conditions. You should feed them regularly with organic plant food and you can make your own plant food by rotting down comfrey leaves in a large plastic bucket. After the comfrey leaves have rotted for about one to six months, dilute the liquid and water your plants with it. It's more fun using the plants that grow around us for plant food and it saves money. If growing outdoors, grow in full sun, grow in rich soil, dig in two buckets full of well-rotted organic matter such as garden compost and keep the soil moist by watering around plants, not over them. Harvest cucumbers regularly so that the plant produces more. If the plant has a lot of side shots you can snip them off, and the energy will go into producing cucumbers from the main stem.

Varieties. The best varieties to grow depend on where you live. There is a big difference growing in the south of England compared to the north of Scotland. The growing season begins a month later in Scotland compared to the south of England, so it is always good to ask local experienced gardeners what varieties grow best in your area. There are many good organic seed catalogues to choose from.

Varieties include Ashley, Bush Champion, Diva, Early Pride and Fanfare.

Carmen AGM are dark ribbed, well-shaped fruits for growing indoors, all female – remove any male flowers.

Femadam AGM ridge cucumber with trailing habit. It yields well outdoors. Do not remove male flowers.

Zeina gives a high yield of short fruits on strong plants, best to grow indoors. All females – remove any male flowers.

Lettuce

I love growing salads, so I love the basic salad: lettuce, cucumber, tomatoes, coriander and rocket. I also like to put sliced apples and lemon juice in salad.

Growing lettuce is easy and enjoyable. To get an early start you should sow seeds in a seed tray. Seed trays can be bought very cheaply from any store that sells garden equipment. In early to mid-March (In Scotland it may be a little later), just fill the seed tray with seed compost almost to the top, leave half an inch, and sow the seeds by sprinkling them on top of the seed compost. Sow anywhere between 20 and 50 lettuce seeds per tray, depending on how much you plan to use, and continue to sow them at two-week intervals, so you have a steady supply of lettuce throughout the summer. After you sow the seeds, cover them with a quarter inch of seed compost which you should sprinkle on the top very lightly. Water using a watering can with a fine rose so that a light shower of water comes from the can; there are watering cans especially designed for watering seeds. Take trays outside to water and start watering off the trays. When you have a fine spray go back and forth over the tray so that the whole seed tray gets watered.

Do not water too much, generally about 15 seconds a tray, and leave the tray to drain outside. You can water indoors if you're careful, but it is best to water outside. Make sure the seed compost stays damp on a sunny window ledge or in a greenhouse and remember to water them every day. When the seeds start to grow, generally in about a week, be careful watering. After about four to six weeks the seedlings can be taken outside and put into a cold frame, seedlings must be accustomed to outside temperatures. If the weather is good in May or June you can plant the seedlings outside without the need for a cold frame. You can even sow lettuce seeds directly into the soil outside in the summer. Make sure the soil that you sow seeds in is very loose, like breadcrumbs, and for lettuce you should make sure that the soil is well-drained, if the soil is not draining well then you can add horticultural sand. Plant lettuce seedlings outside about six inches apart. Carefully transplant seedlings using a small stick, hold them very carefully by the leaves. Do not handle seedlings by the stems, if the stem is damaged the plant will die. Make sure you get some roots with soil when transplanting, firm the seedlings into the loose soil using your fingers. Do not forget to weed very carefully around the plants when they are growing.

Varieties. Summer Butterhead (all year round) Loose Head Salad Bowl, Little Gem, Crisp Head, Webbs Wonderful, Miniature Butterhead Tom Thumb, Bronze Butterhead Continuity, Winter Butterhead Valour.

The best lettuce for beginners or for summer growing is loose leaf lettuce. Loose leaf refers to varieties that do not form any type of head. It matures in 40–45 days, but there is no need to wait that long, you can start thinning and eating within as little as three weeks. Winter lettuce can be sown in September for cutting in April.

Marrows and courgettes

Marrows and courgettes are particularly good to grow because they produce a lot for the area they take up. Some people even grow them on an old compost heap. Marrows and courgettes require a sunny situation and deep, rich soil. When growing courgettes or marrows dig the ground two spades deep, add one bucket of well-rotted manure and one bucket ofcompost. You have many varieties to choose from and you should use the same growing method for both marrows and courgettes.

Plant the seeds in small pots in April, fill the pots almost to the top, plant the seeds sideways then cover with a small amount of compost. Remember to keep them watered. Place the pots on a sunny window ledge or in a propagator. Transplant the small plants at the end of May into their permanent bed and water them thoroughly after transplanting. Fertilisation is normally carried out by insects, but you may want to remove some pollen from the male flower to the female if you are not getting results, female flowers have some fruit behind them. Slugs may be a problem so it's best to wait until the plant has some big leaves before transplanting or go out in the evening or early morning and pick the slugs off. Slugs will not go on copper, so if you can manage to put copper round the base of your plant then that will help. Marrows and courgettes should produce three months after sowing the seeds. Pick courgettes before they get too big, about 4–12in long; you can leave marrows until they reach 2½ft –3ft long. Marrows will last for months in a cool dry room, while courgettes will last for up to a month in the same conditions. Harvest before the first frost.

French beans

Despite their name, French beans originally come from Peru. I love growing them because they produce so many beans. There are two types of French bean: dwarf and climbing.

Plant French beans in light, well-drained soil in a sunny position with a bit of shelter from the wind if possible. Dig the ground in the autumn before sowing and add well-rotted manure or compost, or a bit of both, applying a bucketful per square yard. Varieties of dwarf beans include Canadian Wonder, Cordon and Earl Green; varieties of climbing bean include Blue Lake, White Seeded and Purple Podded Climbing. By sowing in succession,

French beans can be picked from late June to October. Sow the seeds in mid-May or at the end of May in the north, or sow in small pots at the end of April if you have a propagator or a sunny window ledge; be sure to be careful when transplanting and be careful not to disturb the roots. Sow the seeds in drills 2 in (50mm) deep with rows spaced 18in (455mm) apart. Sow seeds 9in (230mm) apart in pairs. Start supporting climbing beans when they reach 4in (100mm) high. I generally use strong tall canes with string or wire to support the plants.

French beans start producing after about eight to ten weeks, be careful not to pull the whole plant out of the ground when harvesting and make sure that you don't leave the beans on the plants for too long.

Kale

Kale is easy to grow, and my favourite variety is called Nero di Toscana. Curly kale is also an exceptionally good producer. Kale is extremely hardy and will provide you with greens all winter. It is best grown on medium or heavy loam which has been well manured from a previous crop. Kale thrives in alkaline soil so you should apply lime after digging the plot during the previous winter. Sow it during April in seed trays with separate compartments, or in a normal seed tray. Fill the tray with seed compost, pat down firmly and sprinkle the seeds, about 20 per seed tray, and cover with a thin layer of seed compost with a consistency like breadcrumbs. Water using a rose with a fine shower. Leave them on the window ledge or put them in a propagator, or if the weather is good just sow outside.

If you are sowing outside then make a drill ½in (12mm)

deep, sprinkle in the seeds and then cover with a thin layer of soil. When the plants have four leaves, thin to four inches apart. In June, when the plants have grown good leaves, transplant them to their prepared permanent bed 2ft (610mm) apart, firm the plants in and keep them well-watered. Make sure you weed regularly and very carefully. Harvest kale all winter, the biggest leaves first so they do not rot, and continue to harvest whenever you need more leaves. At the end of winter, when you have harvested all the leaves, pull the plants up and chop the stems before putting on the compost.

Mint

Mint is very easy to grow and makes great tea. There are different types of mint: peppermint, spearmint, and mint. Spearmint is good with potatoes. It will grow in most soils, so keep the soil moist and add a couple of spadefuls of manure or compost before planting, dig the soil at least one spade depth and break up before planting. Mint will grow in a semi shade. You can grow it in a window box or in a pot if you have a wide ledge.

Mint is easy to grow; sow the seeds in March or April by filling a small pot or tray with seed compost and leave enough room to cover the seeds. Sow the seeds, then cover with a thin layer of compost. Water with a fine rose watering can and put on a sunny window ledge or in a propagator. When the plants have grown 4–6in tall (100–150mm), transplant them outside to their permanent well-prepared bed.

Another option is to get a few roots from a neighbour with a well-established plant in March and plant them in your garden. Ask first, most gardeners are more than happy to help other gardeners out. Plant them 2in (50mm) deep and 6in (150mm) apart. You can also buy small plants from a nursery. Mint will spread, so grow in a large pot. Make sure that you don't let it spread too much. You can grow a pot of mint indoors in winter if you have a wide window ledge, and you can dry the leaves and use them for tea. Enjoy.

Parsley

Parsley is another easy herb to grow. Fruit, vegetables, herbs and flowers are easy to grow, it's just a case of knowing how. You can learn very quickly and if you grow on a regular basis you won't forget.

Grow parsley in well-drained fertile soil in a sunny or semi-shade situation and add well-rotted manure or compost the winter before you sow your seeds. Sow seeds in March, April or May. Parsley is a cut and come again herb, so you can have a constant supply over the summer. Suttons Curly Top and Champion Moss Curled are both good varieties.

Sow in drills ¼in (5mm) deep. Seeds may be slow to germinate so be sure to keep watered with a fine rose watering can. Thin to 3in (75mm) apart and when established thin again to 9in (230mm) apart. You can sow seeds in a seed tray by filling the tray or pot almost to the top, pat the compost down firmly and sow the seeds, 25 per tray. Cover with a thin layer of soil leaving ¼in (5mm) at the top of the tray for water to sit on before it drains. Water with a fine rose watering can and place on a sunny window ledge or in a propagator. Transplant when the seedlings are about 4–6in (100–150mm) high. If possible, take a pot of plants indoors for winter use.

Parsnips

One of my favourite veggies, they are great roasted in the oven. If you want veggies throughout the year, then grow parsnips. Harvest them in the winter. Grow parsnips in light, deep sandy soil and grow them in a sunny situation. Do not add manure to the soil, add compost, though if the soil has been manured the year before then that is ok. Parsnips will fork if you use fresh manure. Long varieties for deep soil are Exhibition Long Rooted and Tender and True; medium varieties are Dobbies Intermediate and Suttons White Gem, while short rooting varieties for shallow soil are Avon, Resistor and Offenham.

Sow parsnip seeds in March, April or May, depending on the weather (April or May in the north) in their permanent situation. Make drills ½in (12mm) deep and 15in (380mm) between rows. Thin the seedlings when they are 1in (25mm) high and sow plenty of seeds, so you are sure of getting plenty of seedlings. You can harvest parsnips in the autumn when the leaves have died back, best to wait for a sharp frost to improve the flavour. When lifting, be careful not to damage the roots with the fork. You can leave the parsnips in the soil until February but be sure to dig them all up before March.

Peas

I love peas fresh from the garden. It's best to avoid windy sites; grow peas in the sun. Peas are not difficult to grow, and they will generally grow without much problem. I grow Kelvedon Wonder (first early), Hurst Green Shaft (second early) and Alderman (maincrop). You can also grow sugar peas (Mangetout). Sow from March to June. There are many varieties of peas to choose from; I generally get a catalogue from an organic seed company.

Peas grow in rich, well-drained soil. Dig the plot a few months before sowing and add two buckets of well-rotted manure or compost or a mixture of both. Use a hoe to make a drill 2in (50mm) deep and sow seeds 2–3in (50–75mm) apart. Make sure that the rows are 18in (455mm) apart. After sowing the seeds, draw the soil over the drills. When the seedlings are 3in (75mm) high, push in small twiggy sticks to encourage the plants to climb and when plants are growing strongly you can put in final supports; you can use stronger, taller twiggy branches or use netting tied to posts of bamboo canes criss-crossed with wire or string. Make sure that your supports are the height that the peas will grow to; peas generally grow about 3ft high (1m), so you can pinch the top off the plants when they reach one metre in height.

Make sure that you water peas regularly, especially when they are small plants. I learnt a trick at one small farm I worked on to get an early start to the growing season: fill a plastic gutter with seed compost almost to the top, plant the seeds and keep indoors. I tie the gutters at both ends with rope to a roof support to keep it off the ground. If you leave the peas on the ground, the mice might eat the seeds.

Peppers

I like growing peppers since they are easy plants to grow and good producers. You can grow peppers on a sunny window ledge, in a polytunnel or in a greenhouse, and they will grow outside in an exceptionally good summer.

Sow the seeds in March in 3in (75mm) pots, fill the pots with seed compost almost to the top, plant the seeds and cover with a thin layer of seed compost. Water with a fine rose watering can and remember to leave ½in (12mm) at the top of the pot for water to sit before draining into the soil. Keep well-watered and place the pots on a sunny window ledge, in a propagator or in the greenhouse if the weather is good. When the plant is 6in (150mm) tall, transplant carefully into 9in (230mm) pots or directly into a bed in a greenhouse or polytunnel. Feed the plants with organic plant food weekly. I make my own plant food from comfrey; see the information on plant feeding in this book. Do not forget to keep the plants well-watered. Support them with a cane which you should attach to the plant with wires.

Plums

I love Victoria plums. They grow well in the Clyde valley here in Scotland, look beautiful, taste great and one tree produces so many plums. Marjorie's Seedlings purple plum can be grown for cooking.

Make sure you have enough space to plant a tree. A bush or a half-standard tree has a spread of about 15ft (4.5m) and some varieties may require a tree of a different variety for cross pollination. If space is limited, plant a pyramid or a fan shaped tree and prune. If you only have room for one tree, plant a variety that is self-fertile. Plant in full sun and in well-drained soil, if the soil is acidic then top dress with carbonate of lime (240g per square meter). Plum trees can be planted from November to March, the earlier the better. Dig a hole slightly wider than the spread of the roots, make it deep enough to allow the soil mark on the stem of the tree to be level with the surrounding soil after planting. Place the tree in the hole, replace the soil from the hole and firm in with your feet. Hammer in a support and use rubber ties to secure the tree. Every winter mulch with well-rotted manure, spread one bucket per square metre around the base of the tree. If manure is not available then use compost.

Potatoes

I love chips, and boiled potatoes with butter are also very nice. It is said that the potato first arrived in Britain from South America in 1586 in the holds of Francis Drakes' ships. More than 150 more years passed before potatoes became popular in Britain.

Potatoes grow best in a sunny situation, and they grow well in most soils. Best results come from ground that has been well manured the winter before you plant; add a bit of compost too, and a bucketful of manure per square yard. It is good to get local advice from gardeners about what varieties grow best locally. First early, second early and maincrop varieties are available. First early varieties for harvesting in early summer are Arran Pilot, which has a floury texture, and Pentland Javelin which has good flavour. Second early varieties for harvesting in mid-summer are Ben Lomond, which has a floury texture, and Kerr's Pink which is excellent for growing in heavy soil. Maincrop varieties for harvesting in early autumn include Desiree, which is a heavy cropper, and Golden Wonder, one of the best tasting potatoes for mash or chips. Majestic will grow almost anywhere. Pentland Dell is a good cropper and is resistant to blight and mosaic virus.

Best to buy seed potatoes from a local supplier, if you're

growing a lot then buy a sack or even a few sacks. Buy them in January, February or March. In February, lay the seed potatoes' eyes up in trays, sprouts will grow from the eyes. Keep the trays in a cool room for four to six weeks until the sprouts from the eyes are ½in to 1in (12 to 25mm) long. If you chit the potatoes this way, they will have a longer growing season and will produce a heavier crop. Plant first-early potatoes between mid-March and early April, plant second-early in late April and plant maincrop in May, a month later if you live in a cold climate. Of course, if you have a polytunnel or a greenhouse and you live in Scotland you can plant the same as in England. Plant potatoes 2ft (610 mm) apart in rows which are also 2ft (610mm) apart. Plant them 4in (100 mm) deep with the sprouts pointing up, the best size for a seed potato is the size of a hen's egg, a large tuber may be cut in half before planting. Cover the potato with soil, make a slight ridge over the line of planted potatoes and when the first shoots appear, draw the soil over them with a hoe as protection from late frosts. Earth up the plants when they are about 9in (230mm) tall, and then again two weeks later. 'Earth up' means to cover the plants with loose soil so that tubers which are growing do not go green due to being exposed to the sunlight. Plant apart and put comfrey leaves in with the tubers when planting to avoid blight, if the potatoes do get blight, then cut the stems off at the base to save the potatoes.

Water the potatoes during a dry spring or dry summer. Potatoes take about three to four months to grow. When the flower dies, wait a month and then dig up the potatoes, make sure you put the fork in the soil at least 6in (150mm) away from the base of the plant, try not to stab the tubers with the fork. Lift the plants from the top. I've had as many as 38 potatoes from a plant but don't be disheartened if you don't get that amount, I'm happy if I get ten good size potatoes from a plant.

Store the potatoes in sacks in a cool, dry, frost-free place. Paper potato sacks will do, or for longer storage use hessian sacks. A dry floor covered in straw will do for storage, but make sure you do not put in any damaged potatoes or potatoes that are beginning to rot in the sacks.

Raspberries

I love raspberries. They are so tasty and it's amazing how there are so many different fruits and different tastes. Grow raspberries in full sun, if possible, although they will grow in partial shade. Try to keep them sheltered from the wind. There are two kinds of raspberries: summer fruiting varieties which produce fruit on the previous year's shoots during July and August, and the lighter cropping, autumn varieties which yield fruit from mid-September onwards.

Grow raspberries in well-drained soil that will at the same time retain moisture; add cow dung or other manure to help retain the water. There is no harm in adding compost. Summer fruiting varieties include Malling Admiral, Malling Jewel and Malling Promise. Autumn fruiting varieties include September and Zeva. Buy certified, disease-free canes from a reputable nursery.

Plant canes in November up until March. Dig a trench about 9in (230mm) wide and 3in (75mm) deep and set the canes 18in (455mm) apart with their roots well spread out. Cover the roots with soil and firm down with your foot. After planting, cut down each cane to 12in (305mm) above the soil. This will prevent fruit being borne the first year but will give the plant more vigour to produce fruit the following years. Apply a mulch of well-rotted cut grass or compost around each plant in April to feed them and conserve moisture. Carefully dig out unwanted suckers and weeds (suckers are new raspberry plants). Water the plants well into summer if necessary. I live in Scotland so there is no need for me to water most summers, in fact we get too much rain even in the summer.

The first July after planting, insert an 8ft (2m) post into the ground at both ends of each row, sinking the posts in 2ft (610mm) deep. For summer fruiting varieties, space three 12–13-gauge galvanised wires 2½ft, 3½ft, and 5½ft (760mm, 1.1m and 1.7m) from the ground and stretch them between each pair of posts. Tie the canes to wires with soft string. Every summer after picking summer fruiting varieties, remove the canes that have carried the berries by severing them just above the soil level. Select the strongest current year canes and tie to wires, spacing them 3–4in (75–100mm) apart. Cut out the remaining new shoots, pull out suckers well away from rows. In February, cut off the top of each cane to a good bud a few inches above the top wire. Autumn fruiting canes do not grow as well as other varieties. Space two parallel support wires 2½ft and 4ft (760mm and 1.2m) from the ground and set cross ties every 12in (305mm) so that the canes are supported without being tied. Cut down the canes of autumn fruiting plants in February. Take suckers in November and increase the length of the bed. Plants begin to deteriorate after eight years. Pick raspberries when they are well coloured all over; at this stage they will come away from the core very easily.

Rosemary

A very nice name for a plant. My friends, Phil and Bert, have a sister called Rosemary. To plant and harvest, just follow the instructions for sage a few pages from here and make sure you label your seedlings so you can tell what's what when they grow. Pick the leaves when you need them.

Rocket

Rocket is a really nice plant to grow, it adds a bit of spice to any salad. To grow rocket just follow the same instructions as lettuce. Rocket is one of the fastest growing leafy greens and you can plant it in the garden or in pots. It is best sown in spring or autumn (it can tolerate the cold) and it will be ready for harvesting in just six weeks. You can pick baby leaves after about two weeks. Do not eat too much rocket since it is extremely high in nitrate, just add six leaves for a one-person salad.

Rhubarb

Rhubarb will grow in most soil. Dig in manure and compost before planting. Dig a hole 2ft square (610 x 610mm) where each root is to be planted. Fork in a bucket of manure and compost at the base of the hole, return the topsoil and add one more bucket of half manure/half compost. If you're planting more than one rhubarb plant, space the plants 3ft (1m) apart. There are a few varieties to choose from; the Sutton is a good choice, but always check out what variety is best for your area. There's a big difference between growing in a warm climate and growing in a cold climate. March is a good time to plant rhubarb. You can also plant rhubarb in October to November. In the prepared ground dig a hole deep enough and place the woody root into the ground. Cover with soil, and firm in with your feet. Water plants well during dry spells.

Forcing rhubarb. When the plants are three years old you can select a few for forcing. For an early crop, use a spade to lift a few strong plants in November and expose their roots to frost. In December plant them the right way up in boxes, cover with light soil and put the boxes in a dark shed or cover with black polythene. For a second early crop, force crowns outdoors without moving them, just cover them with a large bucket at the beginning of February. For a third early crop, put straw over the bed before the plants start to grow.

Remember to feed the plants every year with manure and compost, a bucket of mix for each plant. When you need new plants, dig a good plant up and divide the roots. You can sow rhubarb seeds in April in small pots on a window ledge or in a propagator or a greenhouse. Best not to pick stocks the first year of the plant's life and only pick a few the second year, have fun picking as many stocks as you like the third year.

Runner beans

Much the same as French beans. Prepare the soil well by digging in a bucket and a half of compost or manure, or a mixture of both per square yard. Keep the soil moist when plants are growing, especially when the plants are small. Good varieties to grow are Kelvedon, Marvel and Streamline. Sow in pots during April or outside in May, and if you are planting in pots indoors then be sure not to disturb the roots when transplanting. Grow runner beans up strong canes supported by string or wire; you can hammer posts in and use wire to support the beans. Remove the growing point of each plant when it reaches the top of your support. Plants will grow up to two metres high.

Sage

Grow sage in a sunny position in well-drained soil. Sow the seeds in March or April in a seed tray; fill the seed tray almost to the top with seed compost and sow the seeds, 20 to a tray. Cover them with a thin layer of fine compost and water with a fine rose watering can. Place on a sunny window ledge or in a propagator. Transplant the seedlings to 3in (75mm) pots when they have four leaves. Plant them out 12in (305mm) apart when the roots fill the pots or sow the seeds outdoors in May; transfer to their final positions in autumn. Pick when needed.

Spinach

Spinach is quite easy and great for beginners to grow because it grows very quickly and produces all summer and beyond. You can still be picking leaves right up until Christmas and you can leave the spinach plants in the ground over the winter; they will produce edible leaves the following April. It is best to uproot the plant after the spring harvest. Lord Caitanya, an incarnation of Krishna, likes spinach very much, so it is nice to grow it and offer it to Lord Caitanya. Every plant that is producing fruit or flowers or leaves will take a human birth in its next life as long as you offer the produce to Krishna.

Spinach beet or perpetual spinach is the easiest to grow, you can also try New Zealand spinach. I like to grow perpetual spinach because it never fails, it produces all summer and is easy to grow. Make sure you keep it well watered, especially when the plants are young. Sow spinach in seed trays or directly into an outside situation. Sow in March in a seed tray, ideally with separate compartments. Fill the tray with compost, leaving a half inch at the top for watering, pat the soil down, sprinkle in seeds and then cover them with a fine layer of soil. Put the tray in a propagator for two weeks and leave the plants to harden off (getting them used to the change in climate). Transplant the seedlings outside, planting them 12in (305mm) apart. Make sure that the soil is well fed with compost or with well-rotted cow dung; cow dung takes at least six months to rot. If your soil is half decent then you can start growing in it and improve the soil quality in time. Remember that every plant is a devotee of Krishna so treat your plants with respect.

Spinach can be picked as soon as the leaves are about three inches long, do not pick too vigorously in the beginning, first let the plants grow for a couple of months and then pick every week for three or four months. After that you can pick whenever you need. Do not forget that it is Krishna who is providing everything so please offer the leaves with love and devotion to Lord Krishna.

Chard

Chard is much the same as spinach, the difference is that you can eat the stalks of chard. The best chard I have grown is Swiss chard which produces large leaves with thick tasty stalks. Rainbow chard is easy to grow and looks very colourful in the garden.

Strawberries

You have to grow strawberries if you have a garden since they are so easy to grow and easy to propagate. Grow strawberries in rich, well-drained soil. Add compost or manure, one bucket per square metre during the four to six months before you plant the strawberry plants. Plant from March until September. It's best to remove the flowers the first year so that the plant will produce more the second year. Grow from seed or buy small plants that are certified disease free. To grow from seed just plant a few seeds in a pot of seed compost and water well, place on a sunny window ledge or in a propagator; accustom the small plants to the colder temperature before planting them outside. Cambridge Rival is a good, flavoured variety of strawberry to grow, and Red Gauntlet is a heavy cropper.

Plant 18in (455mm) apart in rows 2½ft (760mm) wide. Dig a hole for each plant 1½in (40mm) deeper than the root system, make a mound at the bottom of the hole and spread the roots over this so that the base of the plant is level with the surface, then replace the soil over the roots. You can put strawberry mats, which are sold by most garden centres, around each plant to keep slugs off, although if you put straw around the base of your plants that usually deters slugs to a certain extent. Cover the plants with netting to prevent birds from eating the strawberries; you can buy netting that's suitable from most garden centres. To propagate, just choose runners from your plants, put the part of the runner where the plant is growing into a pot of compost and peg it down with a piece of wire; you can buy wire from any garden centre. After four to six weeks when the plant has rooted you can cut the connection to the main plant with secateurs. You can get up to four plants from each runner. Keep small plants sheltered until you plant them outside.

Strawberry plants are hardy, I've seen fully grown plants surviving two months under the snow. Plants last about five years, then it's best to replace them with plants you've propagated. Enjoy strawberries with cream and sugar or with yoghurt.

Swedes

Swedes are a very tasty and easy to grow vegetable. When I was a lad, my friends and I used to eat them raw, fresh from the garden. They are very nice cooked in a vegetable rice dish. Swedes will grow in most soil apart from acidic soil. If your soil is acidic then you should add lime. Add compost to the ground in early spring, and sow the seeds outdoors in late May or early June. Sow in drills ½in (12mm) deep, 18in (455mm) apart. Thin the seedlings as they grow with the final distance between plants being 12in (305mm). Harvest them when needed from autumn to spring.

Thyme

The Greeks used thyme to flavour soups. Sow in a seed tray in March or April and follow the same procedure for sowing seeds as sage. Transfer into 3in (75mm) pots when the seedlings have four leaves and plant out in September to a permanent situation, which should be a sunny situation in well-drained soil. Pick leaves when needed. Use thyme in salads. Thyme can also be used to flavour drinks.

Tomatoes

I love growing tomatoes and they are extremely easy to grow. Do not worry if you do not get a great crop on your first try, just keep going and you will improve. A salad is not a salad unless it has tomatoes in it. Tigerella are my personal favourite; they are not difficult to grow, they're good producers and are very tasty. You generally need a greenhouse or a polytunnel to grow tomatoes, although I have grown tomatoes very successfully on my window ledge. This can work if the window ledge is wide enough for the pot and for the base tray. You can grow tomatoes outside if the weather is good enough.

Tomatoes take about three months to start producing so you will need about five months of sunny weather altogether to grow them. Always remember that in your tomato plant there is a living soul, so just like we take care of our material and spiritual lives, we take care of the tomato plant. Make sure to water every day and make sure to weed around the base of the plant. After the plant is a couple of months old, be sure to feed it with organic plant food suitable for tomato plants. The more tomatoes the plant produces the more we have to offer to Krishna, and the more we offer to Krishna the more advancement we will make, and the more benefit the plant will receive. A tomato plant will produce anywhere from 10 to 40 tomatoes. Make sure you feed the plant when the fruits start to grow. Do not over feed, follow the recommendations on the plant food container. Sow tomato seeds in a seed tray, and when the seedlings have got four leaves transplant into 3inch pots. When seedlings are 6in high, transplant into permanent position.

Comfrey is a good natural plant food for tomatoes and comfrey plants grow all over the countryside. Just pick the plants after they have flowered so as to give the bees a chance to get the nectar from the flowers before you pick them. Cut the comfrey plants just above the ground, put them in a container and let them rot, then dilute the concentrate with a ratio of one-part comfrey juice and eight-parts waters. You can vary the mixture depending on how thick the comfrey concentrate is. Grow tomatoes in rich moisture holding compost.

Growing tomatoes is easy and exciting. I love harvesting tomatoes, lettuce, cucumber, rocket and coriander, preparing them into a salad and offering the salad to Krishna before serving them out to others.

You can start sowing tomato seeds from January until the end of April. Fill a seed tray with seed compost leaving about one inch from the top and sow about 25 seeds in it. Cover the seeds with a fine layer of seed compost, and water with a fine rose for watering seeds. Place the tray on a warm window ledge or in a propagator. Tomato seeds should germinate in about seven days, so when the plants have four leaves you can transplant by gently prizing out the roots, remembering to always hold the plant by the leaves. Remember that you're handling a devotee in the form of a plant. Put the plant into a small pot in 3in (75mm) of potting compost and leave room at the top of the pot for water. Let the plant grow for four to six weeks in the pot before transplanting it to a larger pot which it will live in for the rest of its life. When the plant is one foot tall, support it with a cane, or if you have overhead support, you can support it with string; tie the string beneath one of the lower leaves and the other end of the string to a roof strut and twist the string around the plant. The plant will grow quickly so make sure you snip off the small shoots which grow between the main stem and the branches. Be careful not to pinch the shoots with the tomato flowers on it. In this way the main stem will grow very strong.

I plant tomatoes in 10in (255mm) pots, but you can plant in bigger pots if you have them.

You can use a grow bag or plant directly into the soil if you have good soil. Make sure plants are 12–18in apart. You can also plant marigolds around the tomatoes to deter pests. Pick tomatoes when you need them. You may have to support trusses that are heavy with fruit, do that by tying them to an overhead support.

Turnips

I love turnips that have been offered to Krishna. Turnips will grow best on fertile soil, but will grow in most garden soils, in a sunny position. Don't sow on freshly manured ground. Sow outdoors in March, April, and May, depending on the temperature where you live, in cold climates wait until late April or May. Create a fine tilth on the soil you're sowing into. Sow in drills ½in (12mm) deep. Thin the seedlings as soon as they are large enough to handle, to 6in (150mm) apart. Be sure to keep well-watered or plants may go to seed.

Propagator

I've built my own propagator, it's very easy. If you're growing small amounts of plants, you can buy a small propagator from a garden centre. If you're growing lots of plants, best to build your own and put it in a greenhouse. Build a wooden frame 2ft (610mm) wide and 4ft (1m 305mm) long. Make the walls from clear, thin, plastic perspex and make a wooden top with clear plastic perspex and wood. The base is made of wood with a plastic sheet placed on top to stop the sand falling through the gaps in the wood. Put 3in (120mm) of horticultural washed sand in the base of the structure and support the structure with sturdy legs so that the structure is 2ft (610mm) off the ground. Run soil warming cables through the sand, 1in (25mm) deep and 1in (25mm) apart and make sure you spread the cables out so all the area that is covered in sand can be warmed. A propagator can add a month to your growing season. Don't leave the plants in the propagator too long and remember to take the trays and pots out when you're watering.

Chapter Ten

Offering food to Krishna

Offering your garden produce to Lord Krishna.

We should offer Krishna the best and the best is that which we grow at home. If we can offer produce straight from the garden, then Krishna will be pleased. Krishna is a vegetarian, so we don't offer him meat, fish or eggs. It is essential that we offer him preparations which have been prepared and cooked with love and devotion and that we pay attention to cleanliness and detail in our cooking. We don't offer Krishna onions or garlic, instead we can use asafoetida, a spice also known as hing, as a substitute for onions and garlic. We can also offer nice fragrant flowers by offering them to pictures of Krishna and His devotees. It's best to offer to the feet of Krishna or the saints.

If we dig up potatoes or other root vegetables then we should wash them thoroughly. A nail brush is good for scrubbing potatoes, cut off any rough skin then place in a bowl of water. The bowls and kitchen utensils we use should only be used to prepare food for Krishna. The pots and pans we use to cook for Krishna we use only to cook for Him, and we make sure we don't cook meat, fish or eggs in these pots and pans. When we cook for Krishna, we should make sure that we prepare the fruit or vegetables properly and we should also make sure we cook nicely using the right amount of spices. The kitchen should be clean when we're cooking. Once the food is cooked properly, we put the preparations on a nice plate and cup used only for

Krishna. We can offer fruit juice from fruit that has come from the garden. I like to offer Krishna blackcurrant juice. I have a plate, a cup and a glass as well as cutlery put aside in a separate drawer that I use for Him. We place the dishes and cup with the food we have cooked next to pictures of our spiritual masters, Prabhupada and Krishna. We then offer to our spiritual master by repeating his pranam-mantras three times. If we're not initiated, then we ask Prabhupada to accept our offering by repeating Prabhupada's pranam-mantras three times:

Nama om visnu-padaya Krishna-presthaya bhu-tale
Srimate Bhaktivedanta-svami iti namine
Namaste sarasvatate deve gaura-vani pracarine
Nirvisesa-sunyavadi-pascatya-desa-tarine

Then we repeat these mantras addressing lord Caitanya three times:

Namo maha-vadanyaya Krishna-prema-pradaya te
Krishnaya Krishna-caitanya-namne gaura-tvise namah

Then we repeat these mantras to Lord Krishna three times:

Namo brahmanya-devaya go-brahmana-hitaya ca
Jagad-dhitaya krishnaya govindaya namo namah

If we're in someone's home and we can't offer in this way, we just say thanks to Krishna for providing for us. It's best if a devotee only maintains his body with food that has been offered to

Krishna with love and devotion. It's also best if the food is cooked with love and devotion and served with a smile. The mentality of the cook goes into the cooking, so the people who take the Prasadam experience the mentality of the cook, therefore it's best to prepare before cooking by chanting some rounds of Japa. For those who don't know what Japa is, Japa means chanting the Mahā-mantra on beads:

Hare Krishna Hare Krishna
Krishna Krishna Hare Hare
Hare Rama Hare Rama
Rama Rama Hare Hare

If you don't have beads, then you can chant softly to yourself. Chanting the Mahā-mantra is the best way of self-realisation in this age and this chanting will bring out the love in your heart; the most important ingredient while cooking for Krishna is love. Krishna doesn't need the chips or the sweet rice, but he does appreciate the love.

Remember, Krishna does not have to accept the food so prepare, cook and offer the food with humility and love. Pray to Krishna and the saints for the ability to cook and offer it properly. Prasadam is one of the most important aspects of spiritual life, no Krishna festival is complete without Prasadam. Prasadam is a very enjoyable experience. The great devotee, George Harrison, said that the proof of the pudding is in the eating. So, if one wants to experience association with Krishna all one has to do is offer their food to Krishna and take the Prasadam. Satyaraj Das wrote in the Back to Godhead magazine that

Prasadam is the spiritual world in an edible form, so when taking Prasadam we are taking part in Radha and Krishna's loving pastimes. Radha is Krishna's most intimate associate, and they have pure spiritual forms; Krishna has a male form and Radha has a female form. When we offer food to our spiritual master, we are helping our spiritual master to make arrangements for Radha and Krishna to enjoy.

We sing a nice prayer in the morning that goes:

Catur-vidha-sri-bhagavat-prasada
Svadv-anna-trptanhari-bhakta-sangan
Krtvaiva triptim-bhajatah sadaiva
Vanda guroh sri-caranaravindam.

Translation – The spiritual master is always offering Krishna four kinds of delicious food (analysed as that which is licked, drunk or sucked). When the spiritual master sees that the devotees are satisfied eating bhagavat-prasada, he is satisfied. I offer my respectful obeisances unto the lotus feet of such a spiritual master.

So, we don't offer food to Krishna directly, we offer food to our spiritual master.

We sing another nice verse in the morning.

Nikunja-yu no rati-keli-siddhyai
Ya yalibir yuktir apeksaniya
Tatrati-daksyad ati-vallabhasya
vande guroh sri caranaravindam

Translation – The spiritual master is very dear, because he is expert in assisting the gopis, who at different times make different tasteful arrangements for the perfection of Radha and Krishnas conjugal loving affairs within the groves of Vrindavana. I offer my humble obeisance's unto the lotus feet of such a spiritual master.

So, when we offer food to our spiritual master and take the Prasadam we are assisting our spiritual master to make nice arrangements for Radha and Krishna's pure spiritual enjoyment.

Krishna will accept your offering even if you don't consider yourself a pure devotee or even a devotee. All you have to do is follow the simple procedures I've written here, and Krishna will accept your offering. What a nice easy way to make spiritual advancement. It's also very good to involve others in this process, even if someone is helping you grow flowers and fruit and veg and they don't know you're offering the produce to Krishna they make spiritual advancement. We don't taste food while cooking if we're going to offer it to Krishna.

Chapter Eleven

Recipes

These are very simple recipes; I use them myself for convenience and to get the energy to do a day's work. If you want more refined recipes, I recommend books called *The Higher Taste* and *Great Vegetarian Dishes* by Kurma Dasa. However I hope my recipes are helpful, I thought I would put them in because I use them and enjoy the Prasadam. It's also nice to know some easy recipes that you can use with produce from your garden. I use these recipes nearly every day, but some people may not.

Please be careful in the kitchen, especially when deep frying, don't leave the kitchen if you have a wok of oil or ghee on the flame. I'm not an expert cook, but I do cook these recipes and enjoy them, as do many of my friends. Happy cooking, enjoy the Prasadam.

Making jam

First wash the jars thoroughly, along with the lids, dry them and leave them upside down on top of a towel to make sure that they are completely dry. Place the jars on a metal oven tray, open end at the top. Put the tray of jars in a preheated oven at 180 degrees for ten minutes. Place the lids in a pan of simmering water for the same amount of time the jars are in the oven. After ten minutes, take the jars out of the oven and take the lids out of the simmering water with tongs. You can now put jam in the jars.

Basic fruit jam without pectin

To make jam, use strawberries, blackcurrants or plums – if using plums cut into halves or quarters. Heat the fruit and mash with a potato masher. Bring the jam to the boil, simmer for five minutes, then slowly add the sugar. Boil the fruit for twenty minutes, bringing it to the boil over a medium heat, and stirring occasionally. The mixture will start with big bubbles and as the jam cooks the bubbles will become smaller. After twenty minutes dribble some jam onto a plate that you've had in the freezer for half an hour, wait a few seconds then run your finger through the jam, if it makes a clear path through the jam and doesn't fill in then you have a good set. Cook the fruit and sugar longer if necessary. I've cooked the fruit and sugar for up to an hour. When the jam is thick transfer to jars. Cover and cool before moving to the fridge for storage. The jam will last for six months in or out the fridge.

Ingredients
1k of berries
1k of muscovado sugar
2 tablespoons freshly squeezed lemon juice

1. Put a plate in the freezer.
2. Put the fruit, sugar and lemon into a heavy-bottomed saucepan over medium heat and mash with a potato masher.
3. Cook the fruit and the sugar; bring the mixture to a boil, stirring frequently. Continue to boil while keeping an eye on it, stir frequently until the fruit is jammy and thick, about twenty minutes.

4. Check the fruit; check to see if the jam is thick. Take the plate from the freezer and drop several drops of the jam onto the plate. Wait a few seconds then run your finger through the jam. If it leaves a track in the jam, it's ready. If it runs back on itself, keep cooking the jam and test again a few minutes later.

Turn off the heat and transfer jam into clean jars. Put lids on the jars and cool to room temperature, label and date. Store for six months outside the fridge. Very good on toast in the morning, enjoy. If freezing the jam, make sure to leave ½ in (12mm) of room at the top of the jar so the jam can expand while freezing.

Apple crumble

One of my favourite things in life is fruit crumble. I've made so many friends by growing, picking, cooking, offering and serving fruit crumble to people. I like rhubarb crumble and apple and berry crumble. I once found a recipe for fruit crumble on the back of a porridge box, I gave the recipe to my friend Rampa. Six months later I phoned Rampa and asked him if he'd tried the crumble recipe. He said, "tried it? I've had it for dinner every day for the last six months!" Not only that, but he'd also given his friend Alex, with whom he was staying and who he was trying to encourage to be a vegetarian, apple crumble every day for six months. It was rice and dahl for the main course and apple crumble for dessert every day for six months for Rampa and Alex. So, if you're trying to be vegetarian or trying to encourage others to be vegetarian, best to vary the diet a bit.

Ingredients
6 large cooking apples
½ k of raspberries
250g of flour
500g of soft brown sugar.
125g of butter.

1. Preheat the oven to 180c, gas mark 4. Put the flour into a bowl. Slice the butter into six parts and then add to the flour. Mix the flour and the butter with your fingertips, rub the butter into the flour until the mixture resembles fine breadcrumbs and mix it with half the sugar. Put the rest of the sugar aside.
2. Put the chopped apples in a glass or metal oven tray, add the other half of the sugar, and spread the sugar equally over the top of the chopped apples and add the raspberries.
3. Spread the crumble mixture over the fruit, and bake in the oven for 45 minutes at gas mark 7.

Rhubarb Crumble

I love rhubarb crumble. It follows the same directions as apple crumble, and you can add cinnamon to the rhubarb before you put the crumble on top. No harm in adding a bit more sugar than the apple crumble. I don't normally use berries in rhubarb crumble. Always cook rhubarb in a glass baking dish since it may react to metal. When serving rhubarb crumble, add a little freshly squeezed orange juice, just to mellow out the taste of the rhubarb.

Kitchari.

Kitcheri is great to give you plenty of energy to do a day's work in the garden.

Ingredients
1 cup (300ml) of moong dhal
1 cup of basmati rice
One large potato
1 carrot
A knob of butter or ghee
½ teaspoon of cummin seeds
½ teaspoon of asafoetida
½ teaspoon of turmeric
½ teaspoon corriander powder

1. Boil 1½ litre of water in a large saucepan, and when the water has boiled add a teaspoon of salt, then add 1 cup of washed moong dhal.
2. Simmer for fifteen minutes, then add 1 cup of washed rice. Clean and chop the veg and add with the rice.
3. Simmer for a further 20 mins. Stir for the next 10 mins. Add a little more boiling water if required.

Add a knob of butter and stir in, and you can add spices if you like. To add spices, melt three tablespoons of ghee or butter in a small saucepan. Add ½ teaspoon of cumin seeds, fry spices for a few mins then add ½ teaspoon of asafoetida, ½ teaspoon of turmeric, then ½ teaspoon of corriander.

4. Fry for five mins then add to the rice and dhal and veg before you offer to Krishna.

Cauliflower pakoras

I like cauliflower pakoras and tomato chutney. I do a very simple recipe for both. Preparation time – 10 mins. Batter sitting time 10–15 mins. Cooking time 12–15 mins.

Ingredients
1 cauliflower.
1 cup of chickpea flour
1 cup of plain flour
2 teaspoons of salt
1 teaspoon of asafoetida powder
1 teaspoon of cayenne pepper
1 teaspoon of coriander
2 teaspoons of finely chopped and seeded green chilies
About ½ cup of cold water.

1. Combine the flour, salt, powdered spices, and green chilies in a bowl and mix well.
2. Add cold water slowly and carefully until you have a batter that will coat the cauliflower pieces, the batter should be neither too thick nor too runny.
3. Add more flour if necessary, leave the batter to sit for 10 to 15 mins.
4. Heat the ghee or vegetable oil on a medium heat in a wok. After about five mins when the ghee is hot add the cauliflower pieces that are coated in batter and deep fry for about 12 to 15 mins.

5. Turn the pakoras when frying to make sure they are cooked on all sides.

Tomato chutney
Preparation and cooking time 15 to 30 mins.

Ingredients
3 tablespoons ghee or oil
½ teaspoon black mustard seeds
½ teaspoon cumin seeds
1 5cm piece of cinnamon stick
3 whole broken dried red chillies
½ teaspoon of turmeric
12 tomatoes, chopped
⅔ cup of sugar
½ cup of sultanas
½ teaspoon salt

1. Heat the ghee or oil in a large heavy frying pan over a moderate heat.
2. Sauté the mustard seeds in the hot ghee until they begin to crackle.
3. Add the cumin and cinnamon.
4. When the cinnamon darkens, add the chili and the turmeric. Add the chopped tomatoes and stir to mix, over moderate heat, for 10 mins.
5. Add sugar, sultanas, and salt. For a jam like chutney cook for another 15 mins.
6. Serve warm or cold with cauliflower pakoras.

Carrot halava

¼ litre of milk

12 large carrots

2 cups sugar

1. Heat the milk up in a sauce pan until a rolling boil.
2. Grate carrots and add to the milk.
3. Simmer for at least an hour.
4. When the carrots have soaked up the milk, add sugar.
5. Add raisins.
6. Add more milk if required at any time during the cooking.
7. Serve warm or cold.

Quick and easy soda bread recipe

170g/6oz wholemeal flour

170g/ 6oz plain flour

½ teaspoon of salt

½ teaspoon of bicarbonate of soda

290ml/10fl oz buttermilk

1. Preheat the oven to 200c/180c/ gas mark 6
2. Put the flour, salt and bicarbonate of soda into a large bowl and mix.
3. Pour in the buttermilk, mix and make a dough. You may need to add a little more buttermilk if the dough is stiff.
4. Knead for ten minutes on a lightly floured surface. Flatten the dough out a bit and shape it to the shape you want it. Cut a cross on the top

5. Place on a greased oven tray. Bake for 30/35 mins. The loaf will sound hollow when tapped.

Veggie soup

1 swede chopped into 1 in squares
12 curly kale leaves, chopped
½ kilo of pearl barley
2 large potatoes
5 litres of water
1 teaspoon asafoetida
1 teaspoon cumin powder
1 teaspoon coriander powder
1 tablespoon salt
2 tablespoons of ghee or olive oil

1. Boil the water in a large pan.
2. When the water is boiling add the rinsed barley and salt. boil for 15 mins, then simmer for another 15 mins.
3. Add swede pieces, potatoes and kale. Simmer for 30 mins. Add more boiling water if required.
4. In a small pan melt the ghee or oil on a low heat. When melted, add cumin powder, coriander powder and asafoetida. Fry on a low heat for 5 mins.
5. Add slowly to the soup, being careful of splashes. Stir in the stock.

Offer the bread and soup to Krishna, this is a very nice way to please him. I love having home made bread and soup with veg from the garden on a cold winters day.

*A beautiful local garden
I love to pass*

*What a work of art, I love how
the colours merge*

Peony roses

*Sweet William flowers make
beautiful flower borders*

My friend Peter's beautiful small garden in Perth, Scotland, with nice apple trees

A very nice lettuce patch

We've been out foraging

A nice tidy veg patch

*Kale is a good veg to grow
for winter*

A nice indoor spring flower display

*A flower border makes a
difference in a street*

*A nice rose garden in Castle Bank
park Lanark*

*Digging the tatties,
(Scottish for potatoes)*

Seeing a beautiful flower is like seeing a beautiful smile

What a difference flowers can make to a house

Chapter Twelve

Pest control

Organic pest control

Try to grow all your plants from seed, then the risk of bringing disease or pests into your garden is limited. If you're working in a garden which has pests or diseases, make sure you wash your boots before leaving that garden. If you introduce plants into your garden that have diseases it can cost you up to seven years of no potatoes or cabbages. Slugs are a big problem in the garden, if you're growing in pots, you can buy copper tape to put round the pot, slugs get a shock if they touch copper, so they don't slip over it. I've used old copper pipes flattened down to deter slugs; I surrounded all the seedlings I had in my cold frame with them. I've also bought mats for the base of brassica plants which had copper mixed with the material. You can go out in the early morning and pick slugs off and dump them a good distance from your garden, at least 500 yards is recommended. If you dump them close to your garden, they will make their way back again. Frogs and toads will eat slugs so you can encourage them into your garden by building a pond. Ducks will eat slugs, if you're going to keep ducks, make sure you get a breed that is suitable to the climate you live in. Ducks that live in England might not want to come out their shed in Scotland because of the cold climate.

To deter birds, put nets over your brassicas. Cover brassicas with nets from the first day you plant them outside, if you don't, pigeons may even watch you planting them and as soon as you go away, they will eat them. I've seen pigeons that were watching me planting brassicas fly away as soon as I put nets over them.

Use mats at the base of your brassicas to stop cabbage root fly. You can buy mats or make your own, even thin cardboard will do.

Plant marigolds near your tomato plants, the fragrance of the marigolds confuses insects, so they stay away.

Plant carrots one and a half metres above the ground, the carrot fly can only reach one metre above the ground.

Grow in a way that if pests do attack you have enough for yourself after the pests are finished. I've grown a circle of lettuce around some of my plants, so the slugs go for the lettuce first.

Some organic gardeners use Nematodes. Nematodes are a biological control which deter slugs from many plants. All you have to do is add the nematodes to a watering can with a coarse rose, then water the plants with the liquid. You can also use a hose to apply nematodes. Nematodes will kill slugs, so only use them if the slug problem is really bad and you have no other options.

If pests get really bad and you're watching all your hard work being eaten, a little bit of pure soap spray can help. I have used a bit of spray as a last resort at times, although it's not very often I've used it. I've used organic spray on very few occasions and only as a last resort. If we don't use organic spray on rare occasions when our plants are being wiped out, we'll have to buy fruit and veg from people who do use sprays. So best to try to grow without using sprays but use them if you have no other option. When aphids have been having a go at my tomato plants, I've separated them and put them outside for a night and the cold gets rid of the small flies.

A good way to keep butterflies off your brassicas is to put fleece over your brassicas, which will let at least 80% of the light through. You can buy fleece especially for this purpose. Caterpillars can be a terrible problem for brassicas, especially broccoli.

There are a variety of predator insects for sale that you can introduce to your greenhouse to control pests. These days natural predator insects may not be around so much due to our modern lifestyle.

To avoid blight, plant potatoes 18in (455mm) apart and 2ft (610mm) between rows. Put comfrey leaves in the bottom of the trenches you're growing the potatoes in.

New Zealand flatworms may be a problem, they eat the earthworms. If you spot flatworms, which literally look like worms that are flat, put a plank of wood down with a sheet of plastic underneath it and leave it for a week, then check it by lifting the plank and plastic. Flat worms will be attracted to living under the plank so when you lift the plank you can collect the worms. Don't throw them near another garden. Find somewhere where the worms won't do any harm to other gardens and leave them there.

Companion planting

There are plants that you can plant side by side that will deter pests. Plant marigolds near your tomato plants, the smell of the marigolds will put pests off your plants. To attract hover flies, plant limnanthes, commonly called poached egg plant. Hover flies will eat aphids.

Chapter Thirteen

Composting

It's a good idea to make your own compost. Don't use cooked food leftovers in your compost heap, they may attract rodents, and don't add citrus fruit peeling to your compost heap, worms don't like citrus fruit peelings. You may want to add your own worms if there's not so many worms around.

You can make your own compost heap by building a simple wooden frame with two sides and a back wall, or buy a composting bin. If you're using a composting bin, put in a mixture of vegetable and fruit peelings and old plants. If the plants you're composting are tough, like old brussel sprout plants, chop them up with a spade, you can also add grass cuttings but not too much all at once or the compost will go mushy. You can add a small number of leaves if you don't have enough leaves for a leaf mould heap. Make sure you don't put in too many vegetable and fruit peelings all at once, best to add a layer of soil every now and then so that the compost doesn't go all mushy. Best also not to add perennial weeds like docks and nettles. Leave the compost heap over winter and make sure the compost bin is full by the end of August or September. Leave it to rot over the winter. You should be able to use the compost by the end of April or May. It's a good idea to add a bit of lime from time to time as you build your compost heap.

If you're building a big compost heap outside, follow the directions for the compost bin, then just build the compost heap in layers and add lime from time to time. Turn the heap every couple of months by putting the top to the bottom and the bottom to the top. That's easy to do by just moving the compost heap to the right or left of its original position and then back again. Make sure you cover it in winter with black polyethene so the rain doesn't seep through. You can also cover it with carpets if you have any old carpets, which keeps the heat in. If you're using cow dung, make sure it's well-rotted, it has to be at least six months old; horse dung has to be two years old.

To make a leaf mould heap, just gather and rake up old leaves and pile them up in a heap and leave them to rot; leaves will take two years to rot. Leaf mould is very good for your soil. Both it and cow dung retain moisture, while sand helps to drain the soil if you have clay soil. I would say no matter what type of soil you have you will be able to work it if you add the right amount of compost, cow dung, leaf mould, lime and horticultural sand.

At times, I've composted every plant available and any soil that's around. For instance, when I first took over my allotment the soil wasn't very good, the allotment was covered in long grass and weeds, so I just dug everything up and made a compost heap out of it. The allotment wasn't very big, so I was prepared to compost all the weeds and turfs of grass. Because it isn't very big I'm prepared to do a bit of extra weeding. We have to be practical. Weeds rotted down make good compost, and if the ground we're growing on is poor then weedy compost is better than nothing.

We can bend the rules a bit at times. One day I was reading a book, and, in the book, it was written that we shouldn't grow carrots in manure, so I thought "fine, I won't do that". After

I put the book down, I went for a walk around our local village. I like to walk around and talk to people in their gardens, so I went down to speak to a man in our village who has a nice garden and grows fruit, vegetables and flowers. He showed me some carrots he was growing, he pulled a carrot out of a barrel, it was a perfect carrot. I said to him "how did you grow a carrot like that, what's the secret?" He said, "I grow them in cow manure". I said "I've just read a book that advises not to grow carrots in manure", and he said, "there's a secret, sow the seeds close together and don't thin too much, then the carrots won't fork when they grow because they will grow straight down since they are forcing each other to grow straight down". So, we can learn from others who don't always go by the book.

Chapter Fourteen

Be practical

Crop rotation

Crop rotation is essential. If we grow the same crops on the same land year after year, disease can set in. Different crops require different soil treatment also. Crop rotation means that we grow a certain group of crops in a certain area of the garden, then the following year we move that group of crops to another area, and we rotate three groups of plants every year.

There are three groups of crops: brassicas, roots and legumes. It's a good idea to draw up a plan on a piece of paper of what you're going to grow and what size of an area you're allocating to your groups of plants. For brassicas (cabbage, Brussel sprouts, kale, broccoli, cauliflowers) you can add some well-rotted manure the winter before, then add some compost just before you plant, brassicas like a sprinkle of lime too. For roots (beetroots, carrots, parsnips, swedes, turnips) don't add any manure the winter before sowing, compost is fine. Potatoes are the only root crops which like manure, so add well-rotted manure in the ground that you're going to grow your potatoes in the winter before you plant them. Don't add lime to the area you're going to grow your potatoes on. Legumes are peas, beans, lettuce, tomatoes, spinach, chard, and sweet corn. Onions and leeks also fit into this category. Peas and beans like well-rotted manure added to the earth the winter before you sow them. Don't use manure in the soil you're growing tomatoes in. Peas and beans leave nitrogen in the soil so it's good to follow peas and beans with brassicas.

Permanent crops

Blackcurrants, raspberries, gooseberries and strawberries stay where they are year after year and are not part of your crop rotation. Rhubarb, globe artichokes and asparagus also stay in the same place year after year.

Protect your plants from frost

If you plant outside and there is still a risk of frost then you can cover your plants with horticultural fleece which you can buy in rolls from the garden centre, it's not expensive. When your potatoes start coming through the ground, cover them with some soil, this is called earthing up and you should do this anyway, even if there is no risk of frost. Just draw the soil from both sides of the plant and cover the plants with a few inches of soil.

Use a cold frame if your plants have been in your house on a window ledge or if they have been in a heated greenhouse. Just put your plants in the cold frame for a few weeks before planting them outside to accustom them to outdoor temperatures.

Seed saving

It's a good idea to save your own seeds, if you do this it will save you money and give you a lot of satisfaction. To save your own seeds it's best to buy from an organic gardening company. It's easy to save potato seeds, just dig some potatoes up at the end of the growing season, which will be September to October; best to dig them up when the soil is dry. Put potatoes that are at least the size of an egg and in good condition aside in a potato sack made of paper or in hessian sacks. Don't try to save damaged potatoes, they will rot and cause others to rot. Store the sack of potatoes in a cool, dry place and check the potatoes in the sack from time to time just to make sure that no potatoes are rotting.

Saving tomato seeds is also easy. Just pick a good tomato off the plant at the end of the growing season, cut it into four slices and take out the seeds with a teaspoon, put the seeds onto a piece of kitchen paper and place them somewhere warm to dry, above or near a radiator. When the seeds have dried, wrap the kitchen towel with the dried seeds on it in silver foil. Place them in an envelope and write on the envelope what variety of seed they are as well as the date you put them in the envelope. Place the envelope in a cool dry place; if you want to be really safe then place the seeds in a glass jar and close the lid tightly, take them out when you're going to sow the seeds. It's ok to place the paper in the seed tray and cover with soil, the paper will rot.

Saving peas and beans is easy too. Just harvest them at the end of the season, dry them out, put them in a tray and place the tray in a dry cool place until the following season.

To save cornflower and marigold seeds, just wait until the flower has flowered and is past it's best, choose a dry day and then pick the head of the flower, squeeze the seeds out onto a piece of silver foil, wrap them in the foil and then put them in an envelope with the name of the flower and the date they were saved. Place them in a cool dry place until the next season when you want to sow them, you can also put them in a glass jar and seal it, just to be safe.

Don't forget to feed your plants regularly, there are many

good organic plant foods available in garden centres, and it's best to go by the directions on the container. I like making my own plant food using comfrey and nettles. If you have good soil, you don't need to feed the plants too much. So, try to improve your soil as you go.

Dried flowers

I like to grow flowers that can be dried. Statice and Helichrysum are very good flowers to grow for drying and they are very easy to grow. You can grow them from seed in seed trays. Sow in early spring and put the trays on a sunny window ledge or in a propagator. After the seeds have germinated and grown for three or four weeks, put them in a cold frame for a few weeks, then plant them out.

You can grow both of these flowers in a greenhouse or outside. Plant out in fertile soil that has been fed with well-rotted cow dung the winter before you plant. Add compost in early spring, one bucket per square yard. Let the plants grow for about three months and when cutting the flowers, cut them just above the soil. Put the flowers in bunches of about twelve stems, tie a long piece of string around the bunches then hang the flowers from a beam on a roof. A dark dry shed is ideal, although I have hung these flowers in a greenhouse. The flowers should have dried after a couple of months. When they are completely dried, cut the stems to whatever length you want them. Statice and Helichrysum make very beautiful colourful displays that will last at least six months.

A Gauranga gardening story

I lived in a shabby flat in London in 1988 after returning from visiting a friend in Switzerland. My friend Gordon, living downstairs, had let me use the flat while its usual tenant was on holiday. It was a bit of a junkie scene, so I wanted to move as soon as possible. I visited Gordon one afternoon and his acquaintance, Jim, was there to help with some painting. Jim had brought a book with him to show Gordon the type of art he liked; it was called *Teachings of Queen Kunti* by A.C. Bhaktivedanta Swami Prabhupada, and I borrowed and read it. I then decided to move to Edinburgh since I knew it would be easier to get a place to live and a job there than anywhere else in Scotland. My sister Maura also lived there, so I went to Edinburgh and found a room. The jobcentre put me on to the chamber of commerce, and they fixed me up with a job in a lovely garden centre just outside of Edinburgh. I used to turn up for work early because it was spring and lots of flowers were out, and deer used to run around the site.

On one Saturday, I went into the health food shop below my flat and noticed cassette tapes for sale. I had a Walkman, so I bought a cassette called Golden Moments by John Richardson. I'd been to a few events featuring John in London. I'd also seen him at Bhaktivedanta Manor, the beautiful country retreat George Harrison had bought for the Krishna movement. So, the next week, every day on the way to work, I listened to the Golden Moments cassette tape. We sometimes travelled fifty miles in a van to get to a garden and Big Jock, the boss, used to sit beside me. He asked me what I was listening to, and after

Jock had heard the tape about five times, he started calling me Gauranga, so because the boss was calling me Gauranga, the rest of the guys on the squad started calling me Gauranga.

While working there, I used to go to the Krishna temple in Lesmahagow, Lanarkshire, at the weekends and work in the gardens. We used to cut the grass, and I started growing potatoes and cabbages on a small patch of land behind a small building, which was the Brahmachari ashram, where the monks lived. I told the devotees that all my workmates at the garden centre were calling me Gauranga. Most of the devotees living in the temple used to go out to distribute books and collect money in the towns and cities of Scotland and the North of England. The spiritual master instructed the devotees to ask everyone to say Gauranga. We used to put Gauranga posters up too, and we had four service buses painted blue with Gauranga painted in yellow on the buses. So, there were double-decker buses painted blue with Gauranga written on them driving around Glasgow, Edinburgh and St. Andrews. There are many funny Gauranga stories that I'm sure devotees who were living in the temple at that time would be happy to tell.

While working at the garden centre, we made the world more beautiful by creating lovely gardens, and without even trying, all the gardening squad made lots of spiritual advancement. Who knows where writing this book will lead me, and who knows where it might lead you? Life is full of surprises.

Chapter Fifteen

Horticultural therapy

I thought I would go into some detail about horticultural therapy. Many people complain about mental health problems, but gardening can help take our minds off many of these problems. If we're enjoying gardening, we forget about the miseries of life, so I hope this chapter will help readers rise above the miseries of the mundane.

I attended a gardening training course in Glasgow in 1998; two young ladies, who were also twins participated in the study at the same time. The three of us went to Edinburgh for the day and we visited a vegetarian restaurant where we noticed an advertisement for an open day at an organic garden. We went along, and the garden was at the Salisbury Centre in Edinburgh, a lovely place where they teach yoga and meditation. While we looked around the garden, we noticed an advert for Redhall Walled Garden, a horticultural project. They were offering free gardening training, and I also saw in the advertisement that they had a no-bullying policy in the garden; I thought that was nice.

So, I went along to Redhall Walled Garden and spoke to Jan, the manageress; she said I could take part in the project if I could get a doctor to refer me. I talked to my doctor, and he thought it was a good idea for me to do horticultural therapy. I wasn't working full-time, and this was a chance to learn how to grow flowers, fruit and veg properly; most of the gardening work I'd done didn't involve growing fruit and veg. I had grown a bit, but not a lot. It was also a chance to work with others in a way that would benefit the world. I also didn't want to drift back into the drug scene while I wasn't working. Lying around over-indulging in drinking and sex isn't good for mental health. I'd been doing jobs like factory work, shops, restaurants and building sites, these jobs were ok to pay the rent, but I didn't fancy a career in them. So, this was my chance to take up gardening full time. I was forty, and they say that life begins at forty. I can testify that my life became more peaceful and steadier after forty.

The first few months I attended the garden, I worked on timekeeping. I should mention I wasn't taking any prescription or illegal drugs while attending Redhall Walled Garden; I had decided to try to just depend on Bhakti yoga to get me high. The idea with Bhakti yoga is to perform our activities with love, which takes us higher. By higher, I mean that Bhakti yoga helps me to transcend the miseries of worldly life, like stress, anxiety, and depression. If anyone is reading this and does take prescribed drugs, it's best not to stop taking them overnight; better to get appropriate professional advice on how to wean yourself off.

Things went well for the first six months at Redhall Walled Garden, and I had no trouble turning up on time and doing six hours of gardening a day. The staff there were very supportive, and I got on with most other trainees. When I had been in the garden for six months, Jan asked me to come into the office. She told me that she and other staff members thought I was a plus to the garden project, which was so great to hear, it was such a nice compliment, and it gave me a lot of confidence. So, I was benefiting from my time at Redhall, and I'd only been there six months. Laziness certainly doesn't help mental health problems, so it was good to have a regulated working day, and I was doing something I liked doing. I also knew I had a future in horticulture. I had arranged with Prabhupada Vani, the temple president at the Krishna temple in Scotland, to work on the land there, so I knew I had a project to move on to after Redhall.

Redhall Walled Garden was in a lovely situation, it was in the woods, and a river called the Water of Leith ran along the side of the garden. I lived not too far from the walled garden, so I used to walk along a canal bank in the morning to the woods that it was in; that beat being stuck in a traffic jam or being squashed in a tube train while going to work. Sometimes it can feel like we've done a day's work before we even get started in the morning. I used to go for walks along the riverbank at lunchtime, and it was nice to work in such a pleasant environment.

The gardening training at Redhall was top class; the staff took time to train us properly, and no one was allowed to just hang around. Everybody had to work, and if someone had some personal difficulties, the staff took time to try to help them. You know what they say, you can't help anyone if they won't help themselves. Generally, the trainees at Redhall were there to help themselves. I remember when I used to find it challenging to get up in the morning. I used to think God helps those who help themselves, so I would help myself by getting up. I have to be honest, when I got up in that mood, God helped me by arranging for me to meet friendly people. I thought it was good that the trainees who went to Redhall admitted that they were in trouble and were looking for help. Some people went to Redhall just to get out of their flat for the day. Long-term unemployed people could go to Redhall; I remember John, who was at Redhall, and used to live near me; I would give him dried fruit and nuts Prasadam (spiritual food) when we were in the garden. He told me that he and his friends used to go to the Krishna temple for something to eat when he used to squat in London. John said that the guys in the squat who would go to the Krishna temple survived and got out of that situation, but those who didn't go to the temple died. The Krishna temple in London has helped many people, especially young people, passing through the city. When I was twenty, my brother, my friends and I used to go to the temple on a Tuesday or Wednesday night and have a big feast; we used to sing and dance too. We'd give money at the weekends before spending it in the pubs.

The staff at Redhall liked that I had time for trainees who were struggling in life; life is a struggle for most people, but some people can't cope and give up hope. I had time for people who had time for me; if we give someone our time and they don't reciprocate, I don't see the point in wasting time with them. I used to provide the trainees with sweets from the temple; I would get a regular supply of sweets from devotees I met in town. Many trainees liked that at break times people would ask me, "have you got any of those sweets?" If I spent my time serving others, I would forget my own problems. A big part of horticultural therapy at Redhall was cultivating good relation-ships with our fellow gardeners. What's the point in gardening with people if we don't get to know each other, at least a bit? Anyway, it's more fun gardening with people we know and love.

We grew lots of different types of fruit and veg at Redhall.

We had some beautiful plum trees on the south-facing wall and we had some lovely apple trees in the middle of the garden. The apple trees were in rows like an avenue going down the middle of the garden. We had strawberries and raspberries outside. In the polytunnel, we had cucumber, lettuce and tomatoes. We grew peas, beans, cabbage, broccoli and courgettes, and we grew carrots and parsnips. We also made our own plant food from comfrey plants, which grew outside the walled garden. We made our own compost; we just made compost bays from pallets and built the compost in layers, a layer of plants and then a bit of soil, then a layer of plants, a straightforward method but very effective, and our plants grew fine. We had our own allotments. Friday afternoons were optional, so we had the option to work on our allotments or go home. I usually worked on my allotment.

We used to make our own leaf mould; we would make a mixture of leaf mould, compost and horticultural sand to make seed and potting compost. Seed compost is one part compost, one part leaf mould, and one-part horticultural sand. Potting compost is two parts compost, one part worm castings or well-rotted manure, and two parts coconut coir. The potting compost mixture I've given is for hanging baskets and window boxes. I wouldn't use manure when growing tomatoes, so you can leave out the manure if you are growing tomatoes.

We grew very successfully at Redhall; I used to harvest fruit and veg, put them in bags, and share them with the volunteers. I would take any leftover produce and cook it at home and invite garden volunteers and friends round to my flat for a meal. I would cook the produce with love and devotion and offer it to Krishna, then share the Prasadam with everyone in my flat. Most people asked for seconds, so I realised that they liked my cooking. That made me happy.

What I liked about Redhall Walled Garden was the personal touch. The staff took a personal interest in me and my life-style; the trainees made friends with me and asked about how I lived. I guess I was setting a good example. People used to say, "you follow your religion very strictly, don't you?" I would say, "no, go to the temple if you want to meet people who follow it strictly." Looking back, I suppose I was doing alright.

I went to Redhall to learn gardening. I don't think it was an accident that I came across it; I believe it was Krishna's arrangement. Redhall was an excellent project, all I had to do was add Krishna, and the process of Bhakti yoga would be complete. When I first went to Redhall, I didn't think people would take an interest in my lifestyle. I was surprised that people were interested in Krishna consciousness.

The diet at Redhall was very good. We used to harvest fruit and veg, cook it up, and everyone would sit together at lunch-time and eat. All the food served was vegetarian. Diet can affect our mood a lot. When being slaughtered, an animal is very stressed and full of anxiety, and it produces a lot of adrenalin, which can affect our consciousness if we eat the meat. Also, the chemicals injected into the animals are still in the flesh when people eat it. If meat is cooked and served to the public, there has to be a very high hygiene standard. We did have a high hygiene standard at Redhall, but we didn't have freezers; most people were happy with the meals from the garden, so why go to all the expense of buying freezers just to have lunch? I wonder why the government didn't put restrictions on killing animals and meat production when there was so much evidence that the coronaviruses were infecting humans due to our unnatural contact with wild animals.

The Botanic Garden in Edinburgh made an arrangement with Redhall Walled Garden. The organisers of the Botanic Garden offered to take volunteers from Redhall to help with the herbaceous and annual borders, so I jumped at the opportunity to get some training at the Botanic Garden. Tim, our supervisor, was very friendly, he's a diamond. The staff at the Garden were great, especially Andy, a Gauranga man. It was nice to work at the Garden and see the public walking around enjoying the gardens. I thought it was nice that mothers with prams could go for a walk around the Garden together. I know gardens need finances, but if we can find a way to finance parks rather than charge people, it would be nice. I think the government should fund public parks; not so many mothers can afford to pay five pounds a day to go for a walk in the park.

The training at the Botanic Garden was excellent. It was nice to work on the borders and see them in full bloom. It was also lovely to walk around during breaks or after work and take an interest in the other projects there. I used to go to the Garden every Tuesday, and I got a chance to meet with expert gardeners.

Jan, the manageress of Redhall, lives in Peebles, so she used to get a veg box from Acme Organics near there. Jan arranged for me to work at Acme for one day a week, so I used to go there every Wednesday. Zeb and Claire owned Acme; they are a lovely couple who taught me a lesson in hospitality.

I used to travel to Acme from Edinburgh by bus, and for the last ten miles of the journey it was only myself and Bob, the driver on the bus, so I used to talk to Bob about Krishna consciousness. He thought it was nice that I was part of a group, a family. I reminded Bob that he and everyone else is in God's family. I once walked past the bus stop on my day off, and Bob was standing outside his bus, having a break. I asked him if he liked tablet (a Scottish sweet), and he said his wife did, so I gave Bob some tablet. A week later, I got on Bob's bus to go to Acme Organics and I asked Bob if his wife liked the tablet I gave him the week before, and he said, "my wife says you should be making tablet, not growing fruit and veg!" That was a nice compliment, even though I got the tablet from the Krishna temple.

Zeb and Claire used to let me stay in a caravan on their land. They have a lovely house on their land; they also have a straw bale house. I used to enjoy having lunch in the straw bale house; it's fantastic, upstairs, downstairs and all mod cons. There's a walled garden on their land with apple trees on the walls and veg beds on the land; they also had a few polytunnels. We were growing a variety of fruit and veg for the veg boxes, and they also got bananas and other exotic fruit delivered to put in them. Most of the time, I worked on the land. Occasionally I would pack the fruit and veg boxes and go out on deliveries. Zeb and Claire were very hospitable, and they used to invite me into their home to have dinner with them and their two children.

Work wasn't too hard at Acme. It was a bit cold at times in the winter, I remember separating the old dead leaves from the strawberry plants on a frosty day; my hands were freezing. Zeb gave me the option of whether to do that work or not. I don't mind working on cold days; I try to do heavy work at such times to keep warm. Wheeling barrow loads of cow dung is good for keeping warm on cold days.

I met lots of lovely people at acme. I used to work with other volunteers who had been to India or been to a Krishna temple or restaurant. Zeb and Claire told me they had been to a Krishna festival in New Zealand and Australia, so I used to take them down some sweets from the temple.

Wiston Lodge

Wiston Lodge was my next assignment. Wiston Lodge is an old hunting lodge at the foot of the famous Tinto Hill. Tinto Hill can be seen all over Lanarkshire, and many people walk up to its summit. Meg, the manageress of Wiston Lodge, gave me a caravan on the land there. My job was to look after the veg garden. Wiston Lodge is way out in the country, so it was tranquil; I used to like sitting in the garden eating breakfast on sunny mornings. The staff at the lodge were very friendly, and we used to all sit together at mealtimes and eat together. Jan had arranged with Meg to take trainees from Redhall out into the country to help with the veg garden at Wiston Lodge. The trainees from Redhall used to go out to Wiston for three days at a time and work on the veg garden. Jan and Meg were happy with my work, and we agreed that I could go out and stay at Wiston in the caravan and cultivate the veg garden. Here was an opportunity to work on a garden on my own and make a success of growing veg. The veg I grew at Wiston grew well, and I was happy with how the potatoes, chard, cauliflowers and beetroots grew; soft fruit also grew well. This experience gave me great confidence. I could now go on to managing a fruit and veg garden myself.

The doctor

The horticultural therapy course I did was a great success. So, after three years of horticultural therapy, I didn't see the point in going back to a job I wasn't keen on, and I had the garden at the Krishna temple lined up as my next project. I spoke to Jan and asked her to come to the doctor with me. The doctor had asked me to go to her surgery to tell her how the horticultural therapy course was. So, we went along, and I let her know how well it was going and asked if I could have more time to work on the garden at the Krishna temple in Lesmahagow. The doctor asked Jan what she thought, and Jan said I had done very well at Redhall and recommended that I have a bit more time to work on the garden at the temple. So, the doctor agreed to give me more time to get over the difficulties I was experiencing. I was getting a bit depressed at times, and I wanted to avoid taking drugs to cope with the problem, and I knew I could work my way out of the difficulties if I were doing the correct type of work and with the right people. I knew drugs had side effects, too, so that was another reason I didn't want to take medication. I was doing some good mantra meditation, helping me transcend the miseries of material life. I chant the Hare Krishna Mahā-mantra every day for about an hour and a half. The mantra is:

Hare Krishna Hare Krishna
Krishna Krishna Hare Hare

Hare Rama Rama Rama
Rama Rama Hare Hare

The proof of the pudding is in the eating, and you won't know if it works until you've tried chanting. So, the horticultural therapy coupled with mantra meditation worked out for me. Spiritually I'm no different from anyone else, so that combination can work for everyone. You could join a community garden or even do your own garden and start chanting the Mahā-mantra for ten minutes in the morning. I've been down at times, and I put it down to being irresponsible; the doctor did tell me we are all responsible for our actions. Although if we want to help someone, it's good to understand the bigger picture and understand that at times, due to pressures, people do things they don't want to do, so if we take the attitude that someone is suffering due to their karma and just leave it at that, that won't help anyone. If we take a compassionate approach, and don't look down on anyone who's trying to make up for their wrongdoing, and don't hold anything against them, we can help them. If we want help, we have to be open to letting people help us. Trust is an essential aspect of getting help or giving support. If we trust someone, we can open up to them. We don't want our lives broadcast to everyone. It's good to be humble and take guidance from someone who's more spiritually advanced than us. They say Bhakti yoga is based on trust and love. I can honestly say that Horticultural therapy really helped me in life. I just added Krishna to gardening.

The Krishna eco-farm in Lesmahagow.

After working at Wiston Lodge, I rented a flat in Abbeygreen, Lesmahagow, ten minutes' walk from the Krishna temple. I started growing fruit, veg and flowers on the grounds at the temple. The temple has twelve acres of land, so I worked in the walled garden, a couple of acres. When I started growing at the Krishna temple in Scotland in 1989 we only had two acres, so we were expanding. I lived in the temple, distributed books and collected money for the project for most of the nineties before moving to Glasgow to do a gardening course. The money I helped to raise was used to buy land and greenhouses.

In 2006, growing flowers was my first service in the garden at the Krishna Eco farm. We have a beautiful altar at the temple, so we need a lot of flowers every day for garlands and displays. So I started growing marigolds and hyacinths; they are straightforward flowers to grow, and it's easy to make garlands with them. I was also growing cornflowers. They come in various colours, so they make lovely garlands. The combination of marigolds and cornflowers is wonderful. Roses were also a good addition. I also grew gladiolas, which are suitable for putting in vases for display on the altar. We also added oxeye daisies to the presentations.

I was growing fruits and vegetables in the walled garden. I grew potatoes, broccoli, cabbage, chard, spinach, peas and beans outside. Climbing French beans, courgettes, tomatoes, and cucumbers inside. I also had a grapevine inside, which produced very nice, tasty, sweet grapes year after year.

One day I asked some volunteers if they could transfer the

grapevine from one greenhouse to another. I gave them careful instructions on how to dig up the roots of plants without damaging the roots, so they set about digging the grapevine up as I had some work to do in the other greenhouse, and I asked them to bring the grapevine down to me when they had dug it up. It hardly had any roots when they bought me the grapevine, but I planted it anyway, hoping that it would revive. I was doubtful of its survival, but I saw green shoots starting to appear after a while, so I was delighted to know the plant had revived. After all, we were doing Bhakti yoga in the garden, and Bhakti yoga means looking after the plants and treating them all as individual souls by serving them with love. Bhakti yoga means attention to detail, so we should be careful when transplanting small trees and brushes because we want lots of roots on them.

We also had a fruit orchard where we had plum and apple trees. There was also a soft fruit section where we grew black-currants, strawberries, raspberries, and redcurrents.

So, it was a lot of work for one person, but I enjoyed the work, and the things that I had planted were giving us lots of produce. It was working out well; I was doing most of the work by myself, and a few volunteers came along from time to time to help out.

One weekend a guy called Stevie came along to the temple. He liked the garden, and we got on well, so I invited him to come and stay in my flat for a week and he accepted my invitation. So, we worked in the garden for the week that he stayed with me. We worked well together, so I suggested to Prabhupada Vani, our temple president, that Stevie should move into the temple and help me with the grounds, so an arrangement was made for Stevie to move into one of the ashrams at the temple. An ashram is an accommodation building where people interested in spiritual life live. If someone moves into an ashram at a Krishna temple, they have to follow principles like no meat-eating, no drinking alcohol, no illicit sex, rise early in the morning, and attend the temple program.

For the volunteers, attending the temple is optional. Stevie and I decided to follow the complete temple program. We attended the first service at the temple at 4.30 in the morning, called Mangala Aarti, where we sang prayers to the Spiritual masters, chanted Hare Krishna and danced. Then from 5.15 am to 7.00 am, we chanted Japa, which is chanting the Mahā-mantra on beads:

Hare Krishna, Hare Krishna
Krishna Krishna, Hare Hare
Hare Rama Hare Rama
Rama Rama Hare Hare

We had a morning program at the temple to put us in a good mood for the rest of the day. At 7.00 am, the curtains on the altar opened. The devotees played a beautiful song called Govindam, and at 7.30, we sang and danced again to praise A.C. Bhaktivedanta Swami Prabhupada, the founder acharya of the Krishna Consciousness movement. It's inspiring to see beautiful garlands and flower displays and listen to the beautiful music.

Prabhupada started a peaceful revolution and was very keen on devotees growing their own food and flowers. He also wanted us to look after cows and make our own clothes from sheep and alpaca wool. Prabhupada travelled all over the world eleven times between the ages of seventy and eighty years old to establish farm communities.

After we praised Prabhupada, one of the qualified devotees gave a class from Śrīmad-Bhāgavatam, which means the beautiful story of the Supreme personally of Godhead. The devotee who gives the class has to be following four disciplines: no eating meat, fish or eggs, no intoxication, no gambling and no illicit sex. He also has to be authorised by his spiritual master to teach Krishna consciousness.

At 8.30 am, we would go for breakfast which was my favourite part of the morning program. Breakfast consists of porridge with fruit from the garden, toast made from freshly baked bread and jam made from fruit from the garden, and tea made from mint leaves. After all that, we were spiritually and materially ready for the day.

Stevie and I rested for an hour after the morning program and went to work in the garden. We worked all day on the land and had a few chapatti breaks. In the evening, we used to take the vegetables from the garden to my flat and wash them and chop them. We used to listen to CDs by my friend John Richardson while we were chopping the vegetables. We had the odd break to watch DVDs of memories of Srila Prabhupada, and at about eight in the evening, we would take the chopped vegetables up to the temple kitchen, where they were for meals the next day.

So, it was a full day, but because we were practising Bhakti yoga and doing our service with love, we needed only six hours of sleep, and we were up at four the following day for the morning program. So, Stevie and I worked together for a year, then I moved from a flat in Lesmahagow to a nearby village called Stonehouse. My landlord had decided to sell my apartment in Lesmahagow; still, he was considerate and offered me another flat in a nearby town called Stonehouse; the flat in Stonehouse had a garden. So Stevie continued looking after the garden at the temple, and I started to work in the garden at my new flat. Because people had been so kind and helpful while working on different garden projects, I decided to visit other projects to meet people and find out how we could work together. I went to Talhm Life Community, near Lesmahagow, and they put me in touch with Jeremy, who owned an orchard in the Clyde Valley, where we got lots of fruit.

Stevie decided that he wanted to distribute books and collect money; he chose to move to the Brahmachari Ashram and become a celibate monk. After a few years in Stonehouse, the temple offered me a flat in Lesmahagow. I took the flat and resumed full-time work on the temple grounds. The new temple president Prabhupada Prana asked me if I would work with WWOOF Volunteers. WWOOF stands for worldwide opportunities on organic farms. I had mentioned to Prabhupada Prana a few years earlier that I had worked in gardens with WWOOF volunteers, so I said I would be happy to work with them.

The WWOOF host provides bed and breakfast and opportunities to grow food organically, and the volunteer has to agree to work six hours a day, five days a week.

So, I informed Prabhupada Prana that I was happy to work with volunteers. I had an excellent experience working with volunteers on the various gardening projects I had worked on over the years.

I remember our first volunteer, Alison. She was about 23 years old and from England and had just finished studying environmental science. It was January, so we worked in the greenhouse, preparing pots for planting, sweeping, and tidying up. Because I had been on my own for a while, I spoke a lot to Alison; she listened, and we talked a lot that day. It was a perfect first day working with volunteers, and Alison asked many questions the next day about Krishna Consciousness. So, we were off to a good start with the WWOOF program.

Alison stayed three days and then moved on. A few weeks later, two young French men came along; they were a great help and worked hard and were good company. I was impressed at how they followed all the rules and regulations at the temple, stayed in the ashram in the evening, and read books; I thought they set a great example.

Stevie had met a young lady called Eleanor on the street in Manchester. Eleanor expressed a desire to learn some gardening, so Stevie recommended that she come and stay at the Krishna Temple for a week and get some experience. Eleanor was 18 years old and a great help in the garden. Young people bring a lot of life to the garden, and it's great to see them growing fruits and vegetables and flowers. The planet's future depends on us growing food, so young people must learn how to grow food properly. Eleanor and I built our first propagator; we made it from wood and Perspex we had lying around. I was joking with Eleanor that we were working like Laurel and Hardy; it was a bit like that; neither of us had built a propagator before, so we had a good laugh while making it. I like to be a bit light-hearted in life.

The government wouldn't give the temple a grant unless we worked with other welfare projects. So, Eleanor and I went to Edinburgh for the day to ask Jan at Redhall for a reference to say that Redhall was prepared to work with the temple. Jan agreed to give me a reference on the condition that we take some volunteers from Redhall to the temple to help with the garden. I decided I was more than happy to help the volunteers at Redhall. Later in this book, I'll write about the Redhall volunteers' day at the temple.

During the summer, we had a lot of volunteers from France, people wanted to come to Britain to learn English, so it was convenient for them to stay on small farms and work and at the same time learn English. One of our French volunteers, Lorianne, spoke good English. Lorianne worked as an estate agent in Monaco, so she had to speak English to customers. She had come to the temple to stay for ten days; she enjoyed her stay, so she decided to extend her stay for another ten days. She was a good worker and attended the temple every morning. After twenty days at the temple, Lorianne moved on to the isle of Iona. She had only been away for a few days when she wrote back to the temple saying that she missed the devotees, the Prasadam and the flowers and asked if she could come back and stay for a while; I wrote back to her that we would be more than happy to have her back. Lorianne turned up a few days later. She was delighted to be with the devotees, and we were delighted that she was back with us.

I kept in touch with Lorianne, she missed our porridge, so I advised her to offer the porridge she cooked to Krishna. Many people like the Krishna food and miss it when they're not at the temple; anyone can offer food to Krishna at home, and Krishna will accept it if it's offered with love and devotion. Lorianne stayed for about a month and then returned to her Monaco job. She enjoyed her stay at the temple because there were many other young people there; she told me her stay at the temple had revived her youth. Spiritually, we are all eternally youthful at heart. If you like the Krishna food and want to eat it at home and share it with family and friends, follow the instructions I've given in this book to offer it.

We had a young French male volunteer staying with us at the time named Nico; he was full of life and was a great help in the garden. Nico made friends with the devotees and took up chanting Hare Krishna while he was staying at the temple.

The gardening project at the temple was an excellent opportunity for young people to learn gardening and get a taste of spiritual life. We had great fun picking the potatoes; I counted 38 potatoes on one plant, and that's my record. Gardening is great for cultivating friendships. If I grow a potato plant and it produces potatoes, the potatoes get cooked with love and devotion and offered to Krishna. The meal the potatoes are in gets enjoyed by lots of people, then the loving energy produced from all that activity goes out to the world. We were out in the sun, doing something productive, and the whole planet benefited from our actions.

The volunteers didn't only help in the garden; they used to come out onto the street and sing and dance and chant with us. I used to like sitting chopping fruit and veg with the volunteers.

That was an excellent chance to learn about the lifestyles of the volunteers who came from worldwide. I used to take the volunteers to Jeremy's orchard to help maintain the orchard. Jeremy's orchard was part of the Clyde Valley orchard conservation project. So, Jeremy and the other conservation group members were happy that we were helping out. It was good to take the volunteers to other projects and give them experience working with other groups working with the temple. One Saturday morning, Palika Devi and I went to a meeting with the orchard conservation group. We came back with a grant for £500, and we bought fruit trees for the Krishna Eco Farm with the money.

Nico, our French volunteer, stayed at the temple for months, it was great to have him around the garden, and he was taking a keen interest in spiritual life. By this time, I was getting an excellent impression of French people and people from all over the world.

The garden was working out well, and devotees were getting on with volunteers better than anyone expected. Everything we planted was producing. And the trees we already had were producing fruit. We were making more than we had ever produced.

I'm surprised that food and flowers grow so easily; how much food a small piece of land can produce is also surprising. Growing food and flowers can be stressful; what if volunteers turn up in August and nothing has grown? So, we have to make sure that we plant appropriately in the spring and look after plants while they are growing. There's nothing wrong with a bit of transcendental anxiety; our anxiety is that we do our service correctly so that others get free from suffering. We can only do our best and then leave the rest to God.

The temple depended on the flowers for the garlands; flowers cost a lot of money, so the temple saved a lot of money by growing our own flowers. It's also good to offer Krishna the best food available, there's no food better than that which is straight from the garden, so I'm sure Krishna is pleased with the produce. Also, people who visit the temple are happy to see that we grow our own fruit, veg and flowers. It shows them we're not lazy, and children are amazed to see food growing. Some kids don't know that food grows. We should be educating kids on how it grows; I started gardening when I was ten, no one taught me, I just wanted to grow some veg.

The Guardian newspaper did an article about my gardening. I told them I was a gardener in a previous life, that's why I started gardening at ten; they printed that article.

Erica the journalist

That leads me to a story about a charming volunteer that came to stay at the temple; her name was Erica. Erica was a professional journalist, and she came to visit the farm for three weeks. She had an arrangement with a spiritual lifestyle magazine to sell them a story about working on the land at the temple. I liked working with Erica. She'd had her problems in life, like many of us. She wanted to help herself and others, so she had come to the right place. Erica didn't just sit about writing; she helped out in the garden and did her bit.

In Bhagavad-gītā Chapter 10, verse 34, Krishna says that intelligence is the opulence of women. I could see that Erica was intelligent. She had sat at home and thought about how she could write an article that would help herself and other people and, at the same time, make money. I believe God helped Erica, too. Krishna will inspire us from within if we want to help others.

Erica stayed at the temple for three weeks and wrote an article. The article appeared in a top-selling spiritual lifestyle magazine a few months later. Well done, Erica! The article described how we create a pleasant, loving atmosphere in the greenhouses and the grounds at the temple. Erica wrote in the article that I played spiritual music to the plants. She also put my top tips for gardening in the article.

Erica returned to the temple (I mention the temple because we hadn't opened as a farm yet). She wrote another article about me called 'changed man'. The article described how I'd changed my ways; I spent time in a young offender's institution in my wild, more youthful days. When I was nineteen, myself and some friends were out on a weekend drinking session; I woke up in the cells on a Monday morning and was given six months in the institution; they gave me a job looking after the garden in the nick.

That article was also in a top-selling magazine; I remember I went down to the co-op in Lesmahagow and bought it. I'm sure that article helped some people. Some people get into trouble and end up caught up in the crime scene. Sometimes if young people are locked up, they take bad association in the nick and become worse than when they went in. I was lucky; I'd managed to get out of that trap and do something with my life. I'm pleased with the people that have helped me in life; I've worked with the government and the Krishna devotees to rehabilitate myself. By the time I was twenty-three, I was absorbed in the drug scene in the west end of London, the heart of the drug scene in the UK. I appreciate the help that friends and family have given me. A lot of people don't get out of that scene. People like to read about someone pulling through since it helps them realise that they can also get free from trouble. Life isn't easy, but it becomes easier to cope if people support and help each other. Many of the things I saw in the West End were not funny; many young people died in the few years I hung around there. If people get the opportunity to participate in a community garden and make friends, that might be enough to save their lives.

Erica also wrote an article about me and sold it to a national newspaper. The article described how I started gardening when I was ten years old; it stated that gardening was natural for me, and I believed I was a gardener in a previous life. In Bhagavad-gītā chapter 2, text 12, Krishna says that never was there a time when he did not exist, nor you, nor all these kings, nor in the future shall any of us cease to be. Reincarnation is a vital part of the Krishna teachings.

Bhagavad-gītā was spoken on a battlefield five thousand years ago. Krishna was talking to the warrior Arjuna. Our real identity is that we are eternal spirit souls; reincarnation means we transmigrate from one body to another. People often ask if they can fall from their human form into animal life, and the answer is yes, if you behave like a dog, you'll take birth as a dog. If you act like a human, you'll take birth as a human. If you live a godly life, you'll go to God. There are plants in the spiritual world, so if we are a gardener or like plants, we may take the form of a plant when we go back home to the spiritual world. Every plant is an individual soul. We can't underestimate the value of plants in this world; without them we couldn't even breathe.

When I started at Redhall, I never thought I'd end up in gardening articles in top-selling magazines and newspapers. Who knows where this book will lead me? Hopefully, people will read this book and like it. I'd like to work with as many people as possible to create gardening projects and help others add Krishna to their gardening.

Opening of Gauranga Hall.

Working the land had gone well. Local builders did an excellent job of renovating an old barn on top of the hill, next to the temple. So, we decided to have an official opening of the eco-farm coupled with an opening of the new hall. We invited local politicians, and I invited people from Redhall, Acme, Wiston Lodge and Talhm, Jeremey from the orchard, and a few friends with whom I had worked. Everyone I asked accepted my invitation, and the devotees were happy with me.

The big day arrived. It was great to see everyone. I noticed my friend Stevie from Talhm had brought a well-dressed lady with him. I didn't recognise the lady at first, and then I realised it was Kirsten from Talhm, she had made an effort to look good for the event. I couldn't believe my eyes; usually, when I saw Kirsten, she wasn't so well dressed. Kirsten used to be drinking when I visited her at Talhm, so I kept my distance.

One day I visited Stevie at Talhm, and Kirsten told me she had met Tony, one of the devotees from the temple. Kirsten had met Tony (Adhoksaja Krishna) on the street in Glasgow.

Adhoksaja was out distributing books and collecting Laxmi. So, Kirsten stopped for him and gave him some money (Laxmi). Adhoksaja gave her a book about Krishna consciousness. So, after Kirsten told me about the exchange, I became friendly with her. I used to take Kirsten ice cream when I went to visit Talhm.

The opening went well. Everyone that attended seemed happy with the speeches, the music and the feast. It was great to see so many lovely people there. Seeing Kirsten so well dressed made my day. My highlight was seeing her there with Stevie. I sat with Stevie and Kirsten for the feast, and we had a good laugh; Prasadam puts people in a good mood, so often, when people sit down and enjoy Prasadam, they have a good laugh. It was nice that there was a lot of fruit and veg in the feast that we'd picked from the land on the eco farm.

Gazala, a volunteer from India who had been living in London, was at the event. Gazala was a fantastic person; she had an excellent mood towards service. She did a lot of nice work in the gardens, and she also helped out a lot at the temple, cleaning and making garlands. Many of the volunteers liked to make the garlands. I remember Delfin, a young lady from France who used to ask me every day if she could make the garlands. We would pick the flowers from the garden and string them in garlands. We needed about three hundred flowers a day to make garlands; that's a lot of flowers to pick daily. I used to have a reserve of plants if something went wrong with the first batch I planted; I also grew a reserve for the reserves. I didn't want to take chances when the devotees depended on the flowers from the garden for garlands and displays. It was a privilege for me to work with volunteers like Gazala. Gazala greeted our guests on our open day. She was very polite and was up there when it came to etiquette; in my experience, Indian people are very good when it comes to etiquette. I did hear Prabhupada say once in a lecture that love was the highest etiquette. That's a relief; everyone has got love in their heart. I'm not so up there when it comes to etiquette, but I try to make up for any discrepancies with a little bit of love.

We used to work in the garden six hours a day, generally from 9.30 am till 12.30 pm and then from 2.00 pm until 5.00 pm. We would do hard work and weeding in the morning, then easy work in the afternoon, like planting flowers and sowing seeds. It rains a lot in Scotland, so we worked a lot in the greenhouses and polytunnels. One anxiety we don't have in Scotland is that we will get thirsty; it rains too much. In the winter, we would just have to do what was practical.

One day a young lady called Fiona turned up at the eco-farm. Fiona had travelled up from Oxford. The year before Fiona arrived at the eco-farm, she had suffered from Crohn's disease, a severe bowel illness. She had ended up in hospital with the illness and gone down to five stones in weight. So, the disease nearly killed her, she was lucky if she could eat half a slice of toast while she was in the hospital.

Six months after Fiona got out of the hospital, she decided to come to the eco-farm in Scotland and stay for two weeks to help in the garden. Fiona worked hard considering her condition; I gave her light duties in the afternoon; she was so weak she could hardly pull a weed out by three o'clock. She was trying, despite her difficulties.

When Fiona first came along, we were planting cornflowers in the rain. Fiona did well in the garden and got on with other volunteers. After two weeks, she asked me if she could stay on at the farm; I said stay as long as you like. We used to work in the greenhouses together in the afternoons. One afternoon our temple president, Prabhupada Prana, gave me a cookie from a gardening event at Bhaktivedanta Manor. Bhaktivedanta Manor had created a George Harrison memorial garden, and they invited George's wife Olivia to open the garden. She brought top gardener Monty Don along with her to the event. I gave Fiona the cookie to show how much I appreciated what she was doing for us.

After Fiona had been in the garden for four months, I took her over to Wiston Lodge and asked if she was interested in a serious relationship; Fiona said yes. That was a relief; I didn't have to think any longer about what advice to give Fiona before she left to go back home. I was racking my brain, wondering what to say to her before her departure. She had done so well considering her condition when she arrived at the farm. I wanted Fiona to continue doing well.

I just went to Redhall to learn some gardening, and I ended up making lots of good friends and getting married to a garden volunteer.

We had our wedding at the temple, and it was a wonderful occasion. Many of my family turned up, uncles, aunts, cousins and nephews and nieces. Many of my friends from gardening projects came along, as did Fiona's sister and her family, including her mother and grandmother. My brother Gerry was my best man, and my other brother Colin was also there. My sister Maura also came to the temple for the wedding. We had a fire sacrifice in the temple, and our temple president Prabhupada Prana was the priest.

Fiona and I worked hard together and made friends with many volunteers over the years. She is very caring and loving towards me and has been a big plus in my life. We have a spiritual relationship which will result in eternal love. I'll take Fiona to the beautiful garden in the spiritual world. I don't want to come back to the material world after I leave this body, but if Krishna wants me to serve in this world, I'm prepared to come back. After all, spiritual life, Krishna consciousness, is all about love, and love means I do what Krishna wants me to do. It's good to want to return home to Godhead, but it's love if we serve Krishna with no motivation to get free from suffering.

I love growing fruit and veg and flowers at the Krishna eco-farm. It's always good to work with volunteers and go on walks in the evening. It's amazing how things worked out at the Krishna temple in Lesmahagow. When I joined the temple in 1989, I didn't think we would expand the way we did. We started with one house, an outbuilding and two acres of land and have expanded to 12 acres. Hopefully, we will continue to develop into a cow farm. It's been great growing at the Krishna eco-farm; it's been wonderful gardening the Bhakti yoga way. I love gardening, so it's nice to add the spiritual aspect and realise that plants have souls and that they are dear to Krishna. Some plants do more for the planet than some souls in human forms. *Srimad Bhagavatam*, a great book about Krishna, says that there are souls in human form that are just two-legged animals.

The grapevine is my favourite plant at the eco-farm. I love digging up potatoes and admiring how Krishna has given us something we can make chips from. When harvesting strawberries, I think of a devotee for every one I pick; in that way, I'm dedicating the service of picking strawberries to different devotees. I like picking flowers from the garden and making flower arrangements, then placing them around Prabhupada and looking at the flower displays.

My favourite activity in the garden is growing salad, picking it and preparing it, then offering it to Krishna, and serving it out to the garden volunteers and anyone else who has turned up for lunch. It's great to taste fresh cucumber and taste tomatoes like they are supposed to taste. I like to add chopped apples to a salad. I become enthusiastic when I'm picking salad from the garden, all the hard work we put in during spring has paid off, and the fruits are ready to be picked. It's a miracle that we can go out to the garden and pick such excellent fruit and vegetables. Amazingly, we can go out to the garden and get food without paying. I call it the bank of Krishna. Krishna is a wealthy man, and he can supply unlimitedly, and there's no need for anyone to go hungry. If we depend on Krishna, he will provide.

I like picking lots of fruit and veg on festival days and taking them up to the kitchen for the cooks to make a feast for the festival. No Krishna festival is complete without a Prasadam feast. Sometimes we have up to twenty different types of fruit and veg from the garden at the temple feasts.

The devotees who live on the eco-farm property that spend their time on the street distributing books appreciate that devotees are growing on the land. So do the congregation, who visit on a Sunday. I love showing guests around the gardens and the greenhouses. I usually take anyone I'm showing around the garden to the temple shop. The shopkeeper and I are always happy when the visitors buy something from the shop. I've got an excellent impression of Indian people; I've met many friendly Indian people at the temple. After working on the land at the eco-farm, I've got an excellent impression of people worldwide.

I love sitting in the greenhouse in the morning and looking at the beautiful flowers. Morning Glory grows up the side of the greenhouse walls; they are amazing colours. It's amazing how the colours of flowers merge into each other. In Bhagavad-gītā Chapter 10, text 41, Krishna says that all opulent, beautiful creations spring from a spark of his splendour. So, we can realise how beautiful and amazing Krishna is by appreciating that he created the flower. The colours didn't just merge by accident. They say Krishna is the supreme artist. Someone may paint a picture of a flower, and we may appreciate the artist's ability, so we can also appreciate the supreme artist when admiring the beauty of the flower. By the way, Krishna also says in Bhagavad-gītā Chapter 7, text 7, that he is the ability in man. So, when watching football, I shout Krishna when someone scores a good goal.

The day came for Redhall garden trainees to visit the eco-farm. Nrsimha Vallabha and I drove out to Redhall in the morning in the temple minibus. We picked up the trainees and drove them out to the Krishna eco-farm. Redhall is just over an hour's drive from the eco-farm. Twelve volunteers came, and we planted hyacinth bulbs in the big greenhouse; the trainees worked well all morning. We went for lunch at 12.30 pm, and they liked lunch, one of them said: "we'll be singing on the way home after this". We did some more work in the greenhouse in the afternoon, then drove the trainee's home. I didn't hear any singing, but the trainees were in a good mood on the way home. Next time I'm going to start singing; sometimes, when I'm on a bus, I sing Hare Krishna quietly so that the people sitting near me can hear. When I was a boy, we used to go on school trips to the seaside, and we all used to sing on the bus.

When I started at Redhall, the aim was to learn some gardening and go on and do the garden at the Krishna temple in Lesmahagow. I didn't realise that going to Redhall would lead to many friendships and going to so many lovely places with nice gardens. The staff at Redhall were very personable and friendly and went out of their way to help me and others. I was surprised that the staff and the trainees at Redhall were so open to Krishna consciousness. My time at Redhall opened a whole new aspect of Krishna consciousness for me. I'd never worked for an extended period with people that didn't follow the Krishna lifestyle, but I was able to work at Redhall and maintain my Krishna conscious lifestyle. Sam, one of the managers at Redhall, was very accommodating. He started an interfaith group for the trainees who were interested in religion. He arranged for a minister to come to Redhall once a week for an hour, so every Monday afternoon, a group of us would sit and discuss religion. The minister told me she thought I followed Krishna consciousness very strictly, and I said if you want to meet people who practise Krishna consciousness strictly, go to the temple in Lesmahagow. I suppose how I follow would be considered strict by most people. Although devotees understand that

Bhakti yoga is something different from religion, we discussed religion. Krishna consciousness is spiritual life; its essence is to love every soul, even souls in animal and plant bodies. We're also non-sectarian; if you're a Christian, be a good Christian. If someone brought up as a Christian doesn't want to go to a Krishna temple to worship God, then go to a Christian church and worship God.

There's also romance involved in Krishna consciousness, and there are many romantic stories in the Krishna books. Krishna is not against souls in male bodies enjoying with souls in female bodies. I'm not against people enjoying either, so when Phil approached me in the garden and asked if I could arrange for him to work with a young lady called Berta, I was happy to make that arrangement. Phil was from London and had been at the farm for a couple of weeks; Berta was from Spain and had stayed at the farm before; this was her second stay at the farm. They were both about the same age. Phil and Berta worked well together and formed a close relationship.

Phil and Berta stayed at the farm for a couple of months, then went out to Spain, where they got married and had a baby boy. They started growing food in Spain and bought a van, and they now travel around Spain in a van they've converted into a takeaway food trailer. They sell vegan food that they offer to Krishna.

Phil and Berta are a success story of the eco-farm. There are many success stories from the gardening project at the eco-farm. In Bhakti yoga, a little bit of service to Krishna can make a big difference in someone's life. We have a saying; 'a little bit of service to Krishna can free one from the most dangerous type of fear'. The biggest fear a soul has in the human form is falling back into the animal species. The soul in the human form can conceive of God, a soul in an animal form cannot conceive of God. The human form of life is meant for asking questions. If we are in a human form and we don't inquire how we can get free from suffering, then we're not actually human; we're just the same as an animal. Animals don't go to temples and ask how they can get free from suffering. So even a little bit of service can elevate the soul in a human from animal consciousness to God-consciousness.

I like to give people sweets that were offered to God. I always take some sweets out with me, and if I get the opportunity and it's practical, I give people sweets. I give people I work with sweets, I give family and friends sweets, I give bus drivers sweets. I gave a bus driver a sweet once, and when I got back on his bus, he said he thoroughly enjoyed the sweet I gave him. Shortly after that, I was waiting at a bus stop, and the same bus driver passed in a bus; he tooted his horn and gave me a wave. Anyway, not to get off the subject of Phil and Berta, I'm proud of them, I relate to them like they were my children since they are half my age. I would be happy if I had children like them. I haven't got children, so it's nice to have met Phil and Berta in life.

There were so many lovely volunteers at the eco-farm, and I'm sure there will be many more in the future. I've had a great time working with the volunteers; having lunch with them was always enjoyable. I tried to grow fruit and veg to have something from the garden for lunch every day all year round. When volunteers first come along they can't believe how enjoyable the food is, and they say they've never tasted food like it before. The difference between the food that people usually eat and the Krishna food is that the Krishna food has been grown with love and devotion, cooked with love and devotion and offered to Krishna with love and devotion. It also makes a difference if we serve the food with a smile and have a pleasant light-hearted conversation at mealtimes. It's also good to eat in a pleasant environment. Our dining room at the eco-farm has excellent pictures on the walls and flowers on the table; in winter, we have dried flowers that keep their colour throughout the season. A good meal can make a big difference on a dull day. The Krishna movement is famous for good food, and we have restaurants all over the world; we also have farm communities worldwide. Prabhupada always encouraged devotees to grow their own food. Many devotees are keen gardeners; hopefully, this book will encourage more devotees to grow. I can see the world situation getting to the point where we will have no option but to grow our own food.

I enjoy growing fruit, veg and flowers at the eco-farm because I know the temple will use them. Suppose I work for a gardening company; I just have to do the work they give me, which usually involves cutting grass, weeding and hedge trimming. In that case, that's ok, but I feel very fortunate to have an occupation where I can do work I like doing. If I'm not working at the Krishna eco-farm, I'm working in my own garden and allotment. There's no unemployment in gardening; an experienced gardener will always find work, even if it's only for bed and board.

So that's my horticultural therapy story. Very eventful, not what I expected when I started the horticultural therapy course at Redhall. It worked out a lot better than I thought it would. I helped myself and a lot of other people. Krishna helped me. It's worked for me. If you just add Krishna to your gardening, you can rise above the miseries of material life.

Chapter Sixteen

Gardening during the lockdown

I'm so glad I had a garden and an allotment during the lockdowns. My garden had a lawn before the lockdowns, and it hasn't any longer. I dug the whole garden up. I also built a cold frame and bought a small polytunnel. I grew on my window ledges too.

I've regulated my days over the last 30 years. Generally, I get up between 2:00 am and 5:00 am. I listen to beautiful morning prayers first, then chant Japa for a couple of hours. Then I have an excellent breakfast while watching a nice Krishna conscious video. I'm prepared for a day's work in the garden by that time. I read a Krishna book for half an hour and often listen to a talk about Krishna philosophy. In one of Prabhupada's books, I once read that we can train our minds, and I was pleased to read that, having experienced the difficulties an untrained mind can cause. If we do the same things every day at the same time then the mind doesn't have problems doing something; if we laze around for years, it may be difficult for us to maintain working daily. So, we can train our minds, then when it comes to doing a day's work, the mind will fall into line. They say the mind can be our best friend or our worst enemy.

If we want to make the most of practising Bhakti yoga, it's best to rise early in the morning and do our Bhakti yoga practices. So, during the lockdowns, I got up early. The hours from 12:00 am to 8:00 am are the best hours for Bhakti yoga; those are when the mode of goodness is most prominent. There are three modes of nature: goodness, passion and ignorance; passion is most evident between 8:00 am and 4:00 pm, and ignorance is most apparent between 4:00 pm and 12:00 midnight. The modes affect our moods during the day. We're influenced by a mixture of the modes, but a Bhakti yogi tries to stay in the mode of goodness. Bhakti yoga is about love, so we maintain a loving mood towards others no matter what mode influences us. Krishna says in Bhagavad-gītā: strive for yoga.

Gardening is considered a mode of goodness activity, so it's not so difficult to cultivate the mode of goodness while we're gardening, especially if we've put in a good morning's chanting. It's really up to us. Krishna says in the Bhagavad-gītā that "as they surrender unto Me, I reward them accordingly". The reward for doing service to Krishna is that we get more service. So, if we serve Krishna enthusiastically, Krishna will give us lots of service. If we're busy serving, we'll forget all our problems and eventually get free from problems altogether for eternity. Actually, in the higher sense, we don't have any problems; we don't own anything; everything belongs to Krishna. We don't even have a problem; all we have is service. The great Krishna conscious saint Srila Bhaktivinode Thakura just sat in a room and chanted Japa for the last six years of his life. That's very high Bhakti yoga; we shouldn't try to do that. If we're so high in Bhakti yoga, we will do that without difficulty, and it will be natural. Most people can't chant for one whole day; the Bhakti yoga process is gradual; we don't jump to the highest stage overnight, although we can become fully Krishna conscious in a moment, that's up to Krishna. Krishna is above the modes of nature; he's not affected by them; he's free from the influence of the modes, so if we please Krishna, and Krishna wants to free us from the impact of the modes of nature, he can. Of course, we have our everyday problems like paying bills and disagreements and illnesses that we have to deal with, and it's best not to overthink them. We only get involved with the material world as much as necessary.

We're not robots, and an essential aspect of Bhakti yoga is personality. We're all unique individual personalities, and Krishna can relate to every soul in existence personally. It's good to think about what to do in life and how to do things. We should think about what seeds to buy, and we should also think about how many plants we can maintain. We don't want to sow lots of seeds and have too many plants. If we have a full-time job, we just sow a few seeds and keep a few plants. We can be very enthusiastic in spring, and then a few months later realise it takes a lot more work than we thought it would to maintain the plants.

It's incredible how much service we can do in a day. We can do fantastic service if we practice Bhakti yoga correctly, regulate our lives, and manage our time correctly. Many people are amazed at the amount of service devotees like Srila Prabhupada did in one day.

There's a famous story about Bhaktivinode Thakura, a great Krishna conscious saint who was a high Bhakti yogi. Bhaktivinode took birth in India during the British rule of India, and he used to work with the British government. His life was so regulated that he wouldn't waste a minute. He slept very little and rose at the same time every day; he chanted and ate at the same time every day; he even ate the same amount of milk and chapatis and rice every day for breakfast. He would go to his work as a magistrate every day at the same time. Because Bhaktivinode was so regulated, and his mind was so controlled, he could do twice as much work as anyone else. Because he was so efficient at his work, he also wasn't making the British magistrates look very good, and he could deal with twice as many cases as any of his colleagues.

One day, years after Bhaktivinode had retired from court duties, a magistrate he used to work with came to visit him. The man told Bhaktivinode that he felt guilty about something and wanted to confide in Bhaktivinode. The man told Bhaktivinode that when they worked as magistrates together, he tried to stop Bhaktivinode from doing his work. Bhaktivinode said, "think nothing of it. I always considered you a friend".

I like that mood. If we practice Bhakti yoga sincerely, nothing and no one can stop us; we're souls. Krishna says in Bhagavad-gītā Chapter 2, text 17: "That which pervades the entire body you should know to be indestructible. No one is able to destroy that imperishable soul". Krishna also says in Bhagavad-gītā Chapter 2, text 23, "the soul can never be cut to pieces by any weapon, nor burned by fire, nor moistened by water nor withered by the wind". No one can kill us, and even if we lose our material bodies, we can chant in our hearts. So, we have no fear. They say all fear comes from the fear of death, so if we know we're not going to die, we won't be afraid. When Prabhupada first came to the western world, he used to tell the young devotees to chant and become fearless. Of course, we can have a healthy fear of losing our Krishna consciousness. I used that example to prove how a controlled regulated lifestyle can help us in our daily gardening.

So, preparing every morning is essential; it's also good to have a good evening after a hard day's work in the garden. They say your consciousness in the evening will affect your consciousness the following morning. I like to read about Prabhupada's preaching pastimes in the evening; that's a great way to relax and unwind. I used to stay up until 2:00 in the morning watching the Prabhupada memories DVDs. If we become enthused about practising Bhakti yoga, we don't need much sleep. Bhagavad-gītā recommends six hours of sleep; you can sleep more if you need the rest. I don't like to sleep too much; I always wake up after about five hours of sleep, and I don't use an alarm clock. I also enjoy watching Monty Don's gardening programs on TV in the evenings.

If we're practising Bhakti yoga, we should be careful what we watch on TV. The best gardening programs I've ever seen are Geoff Hamilton's triple DVD series, and I thoroughly enjoyed watching those. Geoff is an enthusiastic gardener. If you're excited about gardening, you'll learn; someone else who is passionate will take the time to show you. If you want to learn gardening, don't just read books; go out and find gardeners who will show you how to grow.

It was difficult for some people to keep occupied during the lockdowns. We're all so used to going out and about. To be confined to a house was very difficult for many people. I didn't miss much during the lockdowns apart from the Krishna festivals. I just got up early, did my Bhakti yoga practices and got straight into a bit of gardening. My allotment is about a twenty-minute walk from my house, so when I wasn't doing my garden, I would walk up to my allotment and chat with the other gardeners. That's the good thing about Bhakti yoga, we can live without a lot of worldly enjoyment. I tried to keep my life as normal as possible during the pandemic. I consider loving God to be normal, and there are far more souls who love God than non-believers. It's explained in Prabhupada's books that the material creation is only one-fourth of the whole creation. Most souls are in the spiritual world, absorbed in love for Radha and Krishna.

Chapter Seventeen

The European farm conference

Krishna Eco Farm is one of many ISKCON farms. There are ISKCON farms in many countries around the world. I am writing this section to encourage people to go to ISKCON farms and learn hands-on how to grow fruit, veg and flowers. We also provide training in cow care and cow protection. The best way to learn how to grow is hands-on, and there are plenty of people of all ages volunteering at the ISKCON farms. The farms would be grateful for your help, and it is a fantastic way to learn to grow things and make spiritual advancement. We still grow in a traditional way; we plant by hand and use bulls to plough the fields. We harvest by hand. We do not spray the crops with loads of chemicals. So, if you want an experience growing food with other people then I can recommend you volunteer at a Krishna farm near you, or maybe if you are traveling you can give volunteering on a Krishna farm a go. I have had a broad experience in training volunteers how to grow fruit veg and flowers at the Krishna Eco Farm.

My friend Syamasundara Dasa, a farmer from England, suggested to leading members of ISKCON that we have the ISKCON European farm conference at the Krishna Eco Farm here in Scotland. That means that devotees from farm communities all over Europe meet at an ISKCON farm somewhere in Europe. Syamasundara is an expert in cow care and has been involved in farming at Bhaktivedanta manor for many years.

Syamasundara visits the Krishna Eco Farm often. I enjoyed showing him around the local area here, we visited an old castle and Jeremey's orchard and went on a walk along the riverbank where we had a good chat while walking. Syamasundara was a great inspiration for me. When I was on my own and had just started growing fruit and veg on a large scale here at the Krishna Eco Farm, he and I used to walk around the eco farm and he was impressed with what I was growing, he encouraged me a lot. We need all the support and encouragement we can get in this world. If lots of people start growing their own food and flowers then we can improve the situation in the world, we will use less plastic, people will be healthier physically and mentally, and we will also we will use less petrol transporting food around. If people grow the Bhakti yoga way, we will give more love out to the world. All you need is love. Love yourself for growing the Bhakti yoga way, if you love yourself, you will love others. If we love one another, we will transcend the miseries of material life and be happy. Real happiness is spiritual and real enjoyment is inner enjoyment. We do not say do not enjoy gardening, we say add Krishna to your gardening.

It was agreed by ISKCON leaders that we hold the European farm conference here in Scotland at the Krishna Eco Farm. I suggested to the management here that we invite a local politician to give the opening speech at the conference. Lisa Cameron, our local Westminster MP, accepted the invitation.

On the 7th of September 2018, devotees from farm communities from all over Europe met at the Krishna Eco Farm, Lesmahagow, Scotland. Kala Kantha Dasa, a leading ISKCON farmer from South America attended the conference, Ajita

Dasa from Australia also attended to talk about his success with the WWOOF project in Australia. Smita Krishna, a senior iskcon monk from Sweden came along. Smita Krishna does not only pray and chant mantras, he also works the land by taking part in the ISKCON farm project in Sweden.

I had attended an ISKCON European farm conference a few years earlier at Bhaktivedanta Manor in Hertfordshire in England, so it was nice to see some of the devotees who were there attend the conference in Scotland. I enjoyed watching and taking part in the soap-making workshops at Bhaktivedanta manor, and meeting and listening to devotees from all over the world.

On the 8th of September I took some friends and some devotees who were attending the conference over to the next village where they were having their annual flower show. Local people display the flowers, fruit and veg that they have grown, judges inspect the produce and give bronze, silver, and gold medals. We did not have any of our produce on display because we had just found out about the flower show. We waited in the queue outside the hall, then the doors opened. Lisa Cameron MP was at the door to welcome everyone, she was happy to see us, and we were happy to see her. We walked around the hall, there were lots of impressive flowers and fruit and veg on display. A gentleman very enthusiastically approached me and introduced himself to me as Mark Horsham, Lisa's husband. My friend Trilokesh had met Mark and pointed me out to him. Mark is our local councillor. He said that Lisa had really enjoyed her visit to the eco farm. He gave me his card and said he would like to visit the eco farm.

Mark visited the farm about a month after the conference.

It is amazing what works out when one goes out to do something for the world. Krishna arranges for me to meet people who want to help. I just started growing some flowers and veg at the Krishna temple in 1989 when we had one house and an outbuilding, 30 years later we have twelve acres of land and twenty live-in properties. I do not put the success down to my gardening alone, it's teamwork, I could not have done anything without the association of the Krishna devotees. I am grateful to the many devotees who paved the way for me to grow the Bhakti yoga way. ISKCON farm communities would not exist if it were not for the generosity of the public. I personally had a very good experience distributing books and collecting money for ISKCON projects. I enjoyed taking garden volunteers out with me on Saturdays to distribute books and collect money. A lot of people would like to live a simple life living off the land, it is just not practical for them to do that just now, but I often think the people who do help us and have a desire to live off the land will get a chance to do so in their next lives. According to one devotee who gave a talk at the Krishna valley farm community in Hungary, there is no doubt that the world will go back to people growing their own food and living in small communities in the country.

Mark and Lisa have helped me personally and attended the Holi festivals at the eco farm with their two young daughters. That is what I like about growing the Bhakti yoga way, I get to meet lots of interesting people. Gardening is not an occupation to be done on your own. It is more fun gardening with others and lots of people come to visit gardening projects.

The farm conference was a remarkable success, it is so nice

to meet people from all over the world who are doing something to improve the situation in the world. There is a lot to be said for the simple way of life. We have a saying: "simple living, peace of mind and high thinking".

Chapter Eighteen

Making a living gardening

There are many TV programs about gardening. I've no doubt the gardeners in these programs are very well paid, but not everyone is going to make that kind of money gardening. I really enjoy watching gardening TV programs after a hard day's work in the garden; I especially like to watch Monty Don's TV programs. Working for a good gardening company can be good money, working as a self-employed gardener can be rewarding.

First you must be trained. A company may take you on as an apprentice, or you could work with an experienced gardener. I trained at a horticultural therapy project in Edinburgh. It is good to think about what type of gardening you want to do. There's hard landscaping, that's really hard work. Soft landscaping is also challenging, but there is more planting. You could grow fruit, veg and flowers to sell. Making hanging baskets and window boxes is a clever way to make money if you have a decent size van. You may just want to learn as you go along, and of course you can learn a lot from books like this.

I've also picked apples, pears, strawberries and potatoes at times. That's seasonal work. Picking fruit and veg can be hard work, but the pay is not too bad. You can check out life in farms all over Britain if you fancy working outside for a while.

I have worked for gardening companies; I have also worked on small organic farms just for bed and board. An effective way to learn is to travel around different small farms and do hands-on work. I worked for the Krishna Eco Farm for an allowance and a house to live in. I once put an advertisement in the local ironmongers in our village, I got plenty of work from the advertisement. I talk to people when they are in their gardens. I was living in a high rise flat in Glasgow and we used to use the laundrette, and one morning I went in the laundrette to wash my clothes and started talking to the owner. He asked me what I did for a living, and when I told him gardening, he asked me to do his garden. I was not doing much gardening at that time so I took the job, and he was pleased with my work and put me on to his brother, who put me on to his friends, who put me on to their friends. Within a couple of months, I was working full time. A gardener will always find work, because there is always some gardening to do. Even when I did not have much work, I used to walk around and chat to people who were in their gardens. Doing two or three small jobs a week has got me by at times. Going out to do a few gardens and painting a few fences a week is better than sitting in a flat doing nothing. I always try to make friends with people that I work for. I was doing someone's garden once every two weeks and on one visit the woman asked me if I could paint their house. They went on holiday and left me to paint – never again! There were just too many cupboards, corners, and alcoves. I managed to finish the painting job and got paid for it, but I definitely prefer gardening!

We can grow one or two plants on our window ledge and offer the flowers or fruit to Krishna. We can do gardening as a full-time job, or we can work full time on a Krishna farm. If we work full time in a gardening job, we can work to please our employers, it is good to do a good job. If we work full time as a gardener, we can donate a percentage of the money (Laxmi) we earn to a Krishna conscious cause. If we work as a gardener just to maintain our Krishna conscious lifestyle, we can count our work as Bhakti yoga. An important part of Krishna consciousness is to be honest with Krishna. if we have a full time job and we have a family to look after, then we may just want to donate some money to the local temple. If I am honest with Krishna and tell him that at this time in my life, I just want to donate some money, Krishna will accept what service we do. We may just want to donate money and chant two or three rounds and follow two of the principles and tell Krishna we will improve as time goes on. We can still make it back to Godhead (the spiritual world) in one lifetime, even if we do not follow everything when we start practicing Bhakti yoga, if we are honest with Krishna. Best to go for it and go back home in one lifetime, we have got nothing to lose and everything to gain. Happy gardening, see you in the beautiful gardens in the spiritual world.

Foraging

I love foraging, myself and my wife Fiona go out and about around our local area. We go for walks and search out wild fruit, we visit old walled gardens, and walk on remote pathways; we're always on the lookout for old fruit trees. Be careful not to trespass, and be careful when visiting old walled gardens, some of the brickwork may be loose.

I'm surprised at how much fruit we have gathered foraging in our local area, we picked loads of raspberries, strawberries, plums, apples and pears. We've made jam, chutney and crumbles from the fruit. Foraging is a great hobby, it's such a nice way to spend a sunny evening. I like getting up early in the morning and going out and picking fruit we've spotted the evening before. We also save a lot of money foraging, it's great to have a hobby that saves money.

Part of the practice of Bhakti yoga is to have some recreation. in one sense all of life is recreation if we practice Bhakti yoga full time. Foraging is great recreation, we have a lot to cope with in life so it's good just to go for a walk and spot fruit and pick it and make jam and chutney out of it, of course part of Bhakti yoga gardening is to offer the fruit to Krishna. If we offer the food we've foraged then the plants we've picked from get spiritual benefit. The more plants we pick fruit from the better. If we pick fruit from lots of plants that means that more souls come from plant bodies into human bodies, plants can't become God conscious unless we engage them in service, and the best way to do that is to offer the fruit from the plant to Krishna in the way I've described in this book. A good way to find out where wild fruit can be found is to ask local people, especially local gardeners. Happy foraging, don't wander too far of the beaten track, we don't want you to get lost.

Closing words

I hope anyone who has read this book will add Krishna to their gardening, I enjoyed writing this book. I also enjoyed growing and harvesting the crops. Most of all I enjoyed the Prasadam from garden produce. It is my humble offering to the world. My heartfelt obeisance's to anyone who has read this book.

It's taken me fifty years of growing plants to be able to write this book. Thanks for reading. Happy gardening.

If anyone is interested in gardening the Bhakti yoga way, please contact me at brianmcculloch89@gmail.com

About the author

Brian McCulloch has been gardening since he was ten years old. He has worked in many gardens around Scotland, including a horticultural therapy project, where he spent some time working at the Botanic Garden in Edinburgh. For the last thirty years his main project has been the Krishna Eco farm in Lesmahagow. He has appeared in gardening articles in the Guardian newspaper and top-selling spiritual lifestyle magazine Spirit and Destiny.

Brian has been practicing Yoga for the last forty years.